CHILDREN'S PICTURE
ATLAS

KU-714-831

ISBN 978-1-84135-880-2

Original text by Neil Morris
Illustrated by Illustratori Associati Boni-Galante

Copyright © 2011 Award Publications Limited
Mapping used to create globes copyright © Map Resources

First published as *Children's First Atlas* by Horus Editions, an
imprint of Award Publications Limited, 1995, revised 2003
This expanded and updated edition first published 2011

Published by Award Publications Limited,
The Old Riding School, The Welbeck Estate,
Worksop, Nottinghamshire, S80 3LR

11 1

Printed in China

Award Publications Limited

Contents

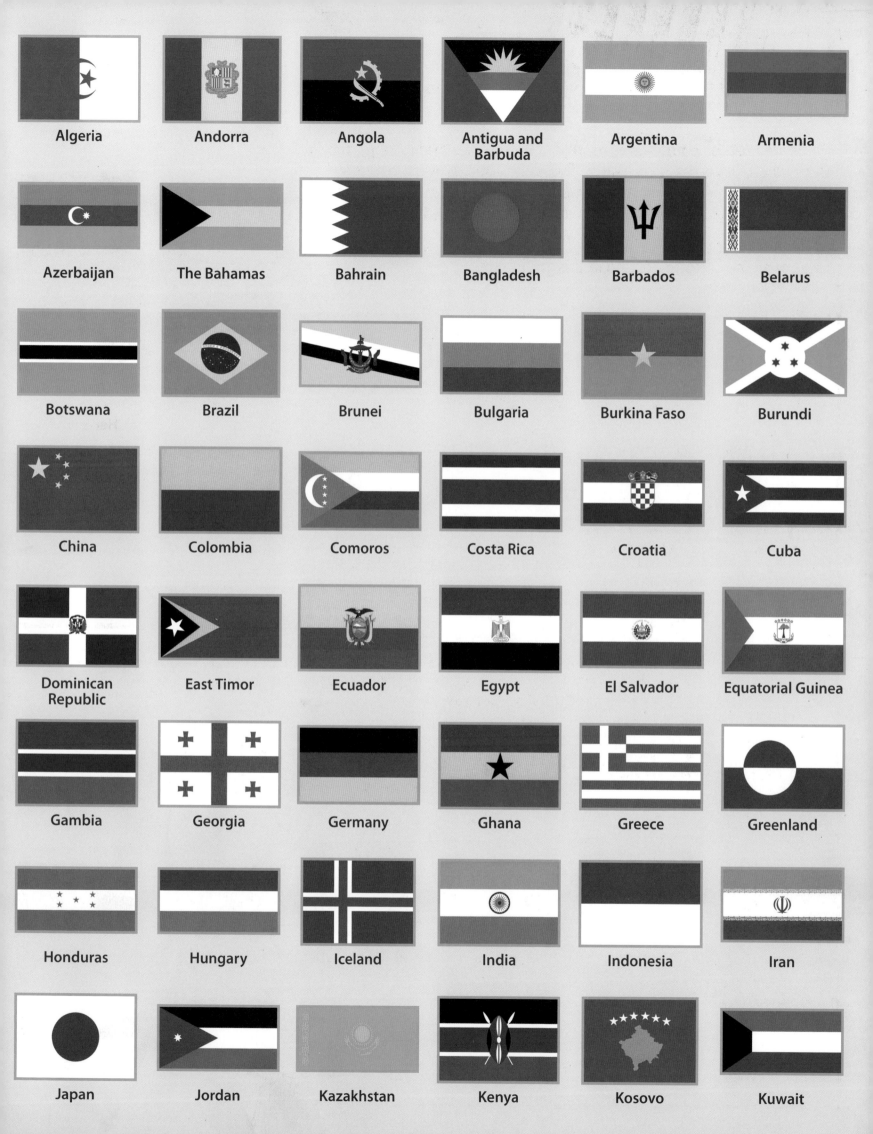

Algeria	Andorra	Angola
Antigua and Barbuda	Argentina	Armenia
Azerbaijan	The Bahamas	Bahrain
Bangladesh	Barbados	Belarus
Botswana	Brazil	Brunei
Bulgaria	Burkina Faso	Burundi
China	Colombia	Comoros
Costa Rica	Croatia	Cuba
Dominican Republic	East Timor	Ecuador
Egypt	El Salvador	Equatorial Guinea
Gambia	Georgia	Germany
Ghana	Greece	Greenland
Honduras	Hungary	Iceland
India	Indonesia	Iran
Japan	Jordan	Kazakhstan
Kenya	Kosovo	Kuwait

How to Use this Atlas

The location of the countries in each section is shown in yellow on the small globes.

High areas of ground, such as hills and mountains, are shown like this. The highest mountains are coloured white.

Seas and oceans are coloured blue. Small areas of blue on the land are lakes. Rivers are shown as blue lines.

Some lakes do not appear all year round but dry up during certain times of the year. These are shown by broken lines.

Geographical features of special interest are identified by symbols such as the one for Niagara Falls shown above.

This atlas is a book of maps and information about the countries of the world. Each map shows an area of the world, accompanied by an introductory text and information about points of interest.

The maps show geographical features, such as mountains, rivers and lakes, that are important to a particular area of the world. Capital cities are shown for most countries, as well as other noteworthy cities.

Symbols represent areas where, for example, fruits and vegetables might grow or where industries, such as mining or fishing, are located. The symbols also show where plants and animals live. Some symbols show famous buildings, and some pictures show the people who live in a region.

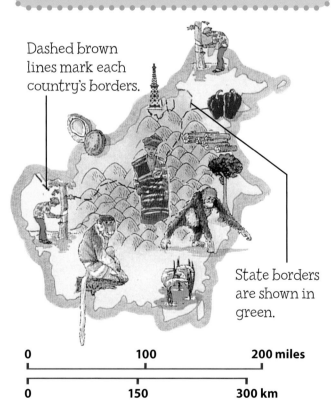

Dashed brown lines mark each country's borders.

State borders are shown in green.

0		100		200 miles
0	150		300 km	

The scale helps you to estimate the size of each country and how far one place on the map is from another. Each map is drawn to a different scale.

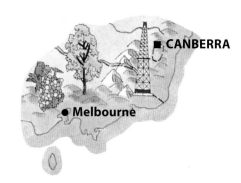
■ CANBERRA

● Melbourne

The names of capital cities are always written in capital letters and are sometimes marked by a square on the map. A dot is used to show other major cities.

Sydney

Some cities are shown by their interesting buildings - like the Opera House in Sydney, Australia - instead of a square or a dot.

Trees of different types show the variety of vegetation around the world.

Spruce and fir trees grow in cold areas.

Broad-leaved trees grow where the weather is warmer.

Rainforest trees are found in hot, wet, tropical areas.

Other symbols on the maps show produce, industry, natural resources, animals, people, or vegetation found in that area.

The World

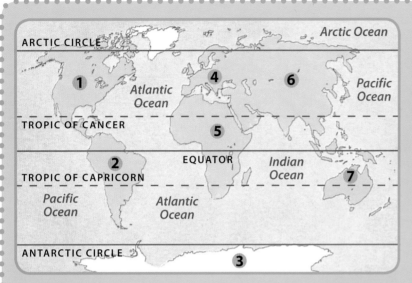

North America and South America make up a long stretch of land between the Pacific and Atlantic oceans. Antarctica lies around the South Pole. Australia and surrounding islands (sometimes known as Oceania) is the smallest continent.

The equator is an imaginary line that splits the world into two equal halves, called the northern and southern hemispheres. It is 40,075 kilometres long. The highest average temperatures are found along the equator.

Around the world, weather conditions, or climate, are very different. A region's climate is affected by its location, height above sea level, proximity to mountains or oceans, and by local winds.

To either side of the equator the Earth is circled by the Tropic of Cancer (to the north) and the Tropic of Capricorn (to the south). Here the sun's position is high is the sky throughout the year. Because of this, days are almost the same length, and countries do not experience four different seasons. Instead, the year is divided into periods that are either rainy or dry. Tropical rainforests are found here.

From outer space, the Earth looks blue, because so much of its surface is covered by water. There are four major bodies of water – the Pacific, Atlantic, Indian and Arctic oceans.

The oceans are separated by large areas of land. These are split into the seven continents of the world. The continents of Asia, Africa and Europe form more than half the Earth's total landmass.

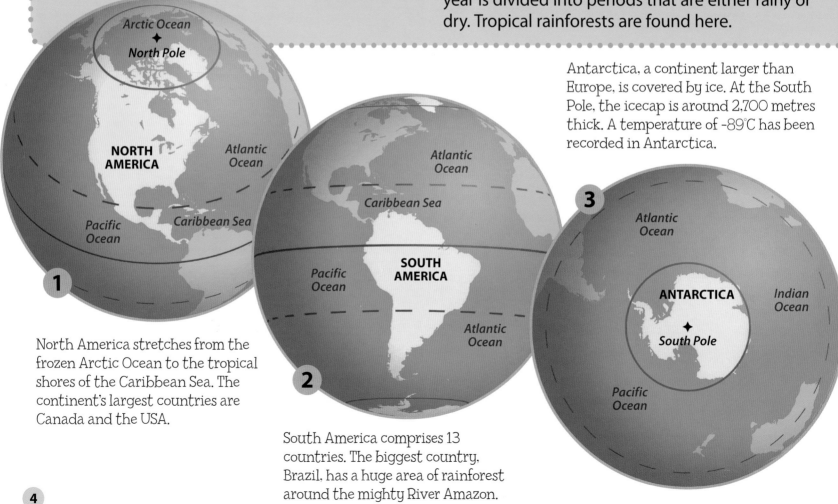

North America stretches from the frozen Arctic Ocean to the tropical shores of the Caribbean Sea. The continent's largest countries are Canada and the USA.

South America comprises 13 countries. The biggest country, Brazil, has a huge area of rainforest around the mighty River Amazon.

Antarctica, a continent larger than Europe, is covered by ice. At the South Pole, the icecap is around 2,700 metres thick. A temperature of -89°C has been recorded in Antarctica.

The Arctic (North Pole) and Antarctic (South Pole) regions are extremely cold. Near the Arctic Circle, the landscape is mostly made up of frozen, treeless plains. The North Pole is in the centre of the Arctic Ocean, where there is no land, just shifting sea ice.

Between the tropics and the Arctic and Antarctic circles, the climate is milder. To the north of the northern hemisphere there are regions of spruce and fir forests, but further south towards the equator broad-leaved trees are common. Warm climates also produce grasslands, such as the Great Plains of North America. A third of the Earth's land area is desert, where very little rain falls.

Except for Antarctica, all the continents are divided into countries. The world's population is not spread evenly across the planet. More than half of all the world's people live in Asia, while no one lives permanently in Antarctica.

Many of the world's towns and cities have grown near to rivers, good soil, natural resources and minerals, which provide work in factories and industry, or good conditions for farming.

Oceania is made up of Australia, New Zealand, Papua New Guinea, and over 20,000 small islands in the Pacific Ocean. Oceania has the fewest people, apart from Antarctica.

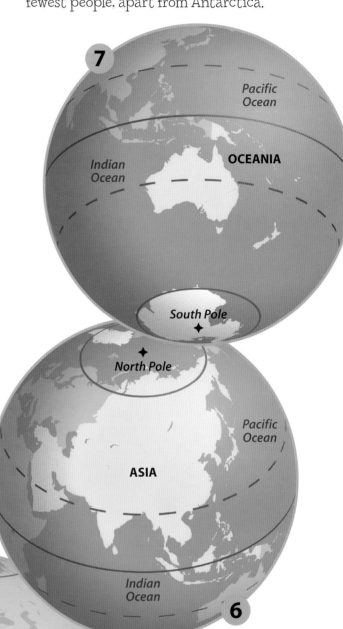

Asia is the largest continent and has the most inhabitants. Russia is the largest country in the world, and China has more people than any other country. In central Asia, the Himalaya form the highest range of mountains on Earth. This is sometimes called the 'rooftop of the world'.

Europe is made up of many countries, stretching from the cold north of Scandinavia to the warm Mediterranean Sea. It includes about a quarter of Russia.

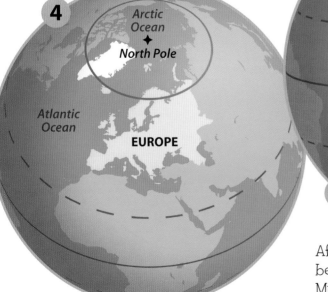

Africa, the second-largest continent, lies between the Atlantic and Indian Oceans. Much of northern Africa is covered by the Sahara, the world's biggest desert.

Northern Europe

The British Isles consists of Great Britain (England, Scotland, Wales) and Ireland, plus many smaller islands. The United Kingdom is a country made up of Great Britain and Northern Ireland. The southern part of Ireland (the Republic of Ireland, or Eire) is an independent country. Cows and sheep graze on pastures all over the British Isles. Oil and gas are found in the North Sea off the coast of Scotland.

Norway, Sweden, Denmark, Finland and Iceland make up Scandinavia. Huge forests in Scandinavia provide wood to make paper and furniture. These countries also have large fishing fleets.

Greenland, a country which is part of the kingdom of Denmark, is a large island. Most of it lies within the Arctic Circle. Few people live there. It is the largest island in the world that is not a continent.

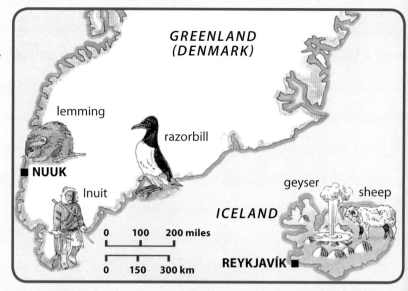

GREENLAND (DENMARK)

lemming

razorbill

■ NUUK

Inuit

geyser

sheep

ICELAND

0 100 200 miles

0 150 300 km

REYKJAVÍK ■

More About...

Hot **geysers** spring up from beneath the frozen earth in Iceland.

Tweed is a thick wool cloth from Scotland, used to make clothes.

Big Ben is a 13.8 tonne bell in the clock tower of Westminster, London.

Hadrian's Wall was built by the ancient Romans across northern England.

tweed

sheep

cattle

barley

oil rig

gas fields

fishing

thatched-roof cottage

red deer

SCOTLAND

North Sea

pony

croft

BELFAST

Glasgow

EDINBURGH

potatoes

potatoes

NORTHERN IRELAND

Hadrian's Wall

oil rig

fishing

Shannon

IRELAND

● Newcastle upon Tyne

pigs

peat

beef cattle

■ DUBLIN

Irish Sea

UNITED KINGDOM

crystal

Blackpool Tower

currach

● Manchester

sugar beets

puffin

Conwy Castle

coal

fishing

Atlantic Ocean

Birmingham

WALES

Trent

fishing

gas fields

seaport

coal

ENGLAND

Oxford

fishing

Cardiff ●

Severn

flowers

barley

Big Ben

wheat

0 100 200 miles

0 150 300 km

Thames

LONDON

hops

naval ship

Southampton ●

seaport

Channel Tunnel

Did You Know?

- There are almost 190,000 lakes in Finland.

- At Legoland in the Danish town of Billund, more than 58 million Lego bricks are used to make model statues, buildings and animals.

- Norway is more than twice as large as England, but England has over 12 times as many people.

hooded seal

capercaillie

Narvik

birch trees

R U S S I A

reindeer

fishing

seaport

Lapp people

musk ox

reindeer

floatplane

razorbill

mining

reindeer

wolf

lemming

otter

lynx

mining

golden eagle

mining

F I N L A N D

fishing

salmon

wolverine

cross-country skiing

Trondheim

skiing

timber

timber

oats

sauna

timber

pigs

stave church

Gulf of Bothnia

cathedral

N O R W A Y

national costume

pigs

rgen

potatoes

OSLO

oats

Uppsala University

oats

trout

sheep

dairy cattle

elk

HELSINKI

Gulf of Finland

herring

STOCKHOLM

S W E D E N

fishing

ferry

Gothenburg

ice-breaking ship

potatoes

dairy cattle

rune stone

eider duck

potatoes

Little Mermaid

rye

pigs

D E N M A R K

B a l t i c   S e a

COPENHAGEN

windmill

G E R M A N Y

More About...

Cross-country skiing is popular in the snowy countries of Scandinavia.

A **sauna** is a steam bath. Finnish people often run outside in the snow after a sauna!

The **Little Mermaid** statue is perched on rocks in the harbour of Copenhagen, Denmark.

Built more than 700 years ago, Norwegian **stave churches** are made of wood.

France and the Low Countries

France is the largest country in western Europe. It has rich farmlands, and its mild climate is ideal for growing wheat, maize and barley. Grapes also grow here, and French wine is world famous. France is also well known for its fine food.

There are many beautiful French cities. Paris, the capital, is an important centre of art and learning. The main industrial region lies north of Paris. The Alps, in the south of France, are popular for climbing and skiing. The Côte d'Azur (or French Riviera) along the Mediterranean coast is a region with many beach resorts.

The Low Countries consist of Belgium, Luxembourg and the Netherlands. One third of the Netherlands is below sea level. The highest point in the country is about 320 metres.

More About...

Truffles are valuable mushroom-like plants that grow underground and have a special taste. Pigs and dogs are used to find them.

The beautiful **cave paintings** at Lascaux may be 17,000 years old. They show horses, deer and other animals as well as human figures.

Basque shepherds speak their own language and live in the foothills of the Pyrenees mountains in northern Spain and south-western France.

In the Netherlands, **windmills** were used in the past to pump floodwater from the land. Dykes have been built to keep the land dry.

The **Tour de France** is the best-known bicycle race in the world. Cyclists from many countries race, covering around 3,500 kilometres in three weeks.

TGV high-speed trains run from Paris to other French cities. They are amongst the fastest passenger trains in the world.

Did You Know?

- France, Belgium, the Netherlands and Luxembourg are all in the European Union. The EU aims to improve life in member countries and helps them do business with each other.

- Belgium has two groups of native people. Flemings speak Flemish, a form of Dutch, and Walloons, who speak a French dialect.

- Luxembourg is also the name of the country's capital city.

- Belgium has the highest density of roads and railways in the world.

- France is the most visited country in the world.

- The city of Amsterdam, in the Netherlands, is built on about 100 islands, which are joined by a series of canals. At least 50 cars a year fall into the canals. There are special police to recover sunken cars and bikes.

Atlantic Ocean

0		100		200 miles

0		150		300 km

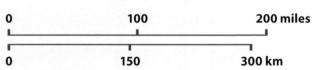

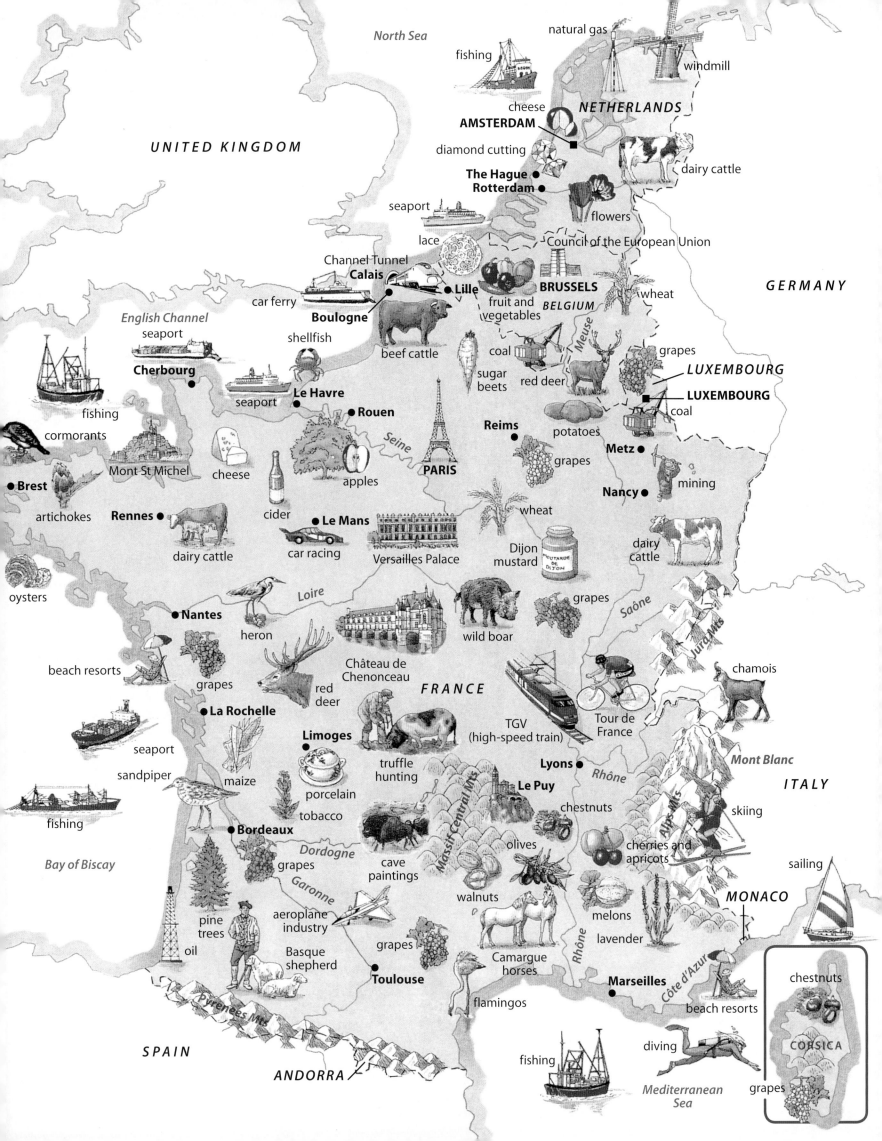

North Sea

fishing

natural gas

windmill

NETHERLANDS

cheese

AMSTERDAM

diamond cutting

dairy cattle

UNITED KINGDOM

The Hague
Rotterdam

seaport

flowers

Council of the European Union

lace

Channel Tunnel

GERMANY

Calais

Lille

car ferry

Boulogne

BRUSSELS

fruit and vegetables

BELGIUM

wheat

Meuse

grapes

LUXEMBOURG

beef cattle

coal

red deer

LUXEMBOURG

English Channel

seaport

shellfish

sugar beets

potatoes

coal

Cherbourg

fishing

seaport

Le Havre

Rouen

Reims

grapes

Metz

cormorants

Seine

PARIS

mining

Mont St Michel

cheese

apples

grapes

Nancy

Brest

cider

Le Mans

wheat

dairy cattle

artichokes

Rennes

dairy cattle

car racing

Versailles Palace

Dijon mustard

MOUTARDE DE DIJON

oysters

Loire

Nantes

heron

Château de Chenonceau

wild boar

grapes

Saône

Jura Mts

chamois

beach resorts

grapes

red deer

FRANCE

La Rochelle

seaport

sandpiper

maize

Limoges

truffle hunting

porcelain

tobacco

TGV (high-speed train)

Tour de France

Lyons

Rhône

Le Puy

chestnuts

Mont Blanc

skiing

ITALY

fishing

Bay of Biscay

Bordeaux

Dordogne

grapes

Garonne

cave paintings

Massif Central Mts

olives

walnuts

Alps Mts

cherries and apricots

sailing

MONACO

pine trees

oil

aeroplane industry

Basque shepherd

grapes

Toulouse

Camargue horses

melons

lavender

Marseilles

Côte d'Azur

beach resorts

chestnuts

SPAIN

Pyrenees Mts

flamingos

diving

CORSICA

ANDORRA

fishing

grapes

Mediterranean Sea

Central Europe

Germany is a leading industrial nation in central Europe. The Ruhr valley is a region of heavy industry, and the river Rhine is an important route for transporting cargo. Northern Germany has plains with fertile farmland. Southern Germany has mountains and forests. Farther south are the countries of Switzerland and Austria. They are overlooked by the mountains of the Alps.

To the east lie the Czech Republic, Slovakia and Poland. They are rich in natural resources and have large industries. Poland has steel and shipbuilding centres on the Baltic Sea. Farming is also important in these countries.

More About...

 The **chamois** is a wild antelope the size of a goat. It lives in the mountains and eats herbs, flowers and pine shoots.

 Bohemia is a region of the Czech Republic that is popular with tourists. **Bohemian glassware** is made there.

 Bison were once found throughout Europe. Now only a few are left. Most live in a protected forest in Poland.

 Switzerland is famous for its watchmaking. Swiss **watches** and clocks are popular all over the world.

 Lipizzaner horses are trained at the Spanish Riding School in Vienna, Austria and perform in shows that are world famous.

 Neuschwanstein Castle in Bavaria was built over 100 years ago for King Ludwig II.

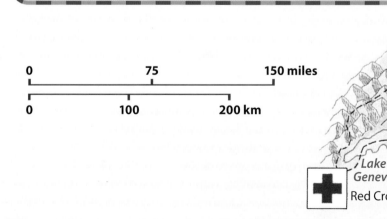

0 — 75 — 150 miles

0 — 100 — 200 km

fishing

Kiel
seaport
seaport
pigs
Lübeck
Hamburg
oil
Elbe
Ho
G

sheep
natural gas
mining
Hannover
salt
barley

apples
sugar beets

Rhine
coal
racing pigeon
Weser

Cologne
mining
half-timbered houses

Bonn
Cologne Cathedral
beer
grapes

wine
Frankfurt
grapes

grapes
GERMANY
market

Trier
castle
grapes
Nuremberg

FRANCE
Dinkelsbühler Boys Orchestra

Stuttgart
buzzard
hops

Black Forest
Danube
Munich
dairy cattl

Neuschwanstein Castle

watches
Zurich
Bodensee

BERN
cheese
chocolate
VADUZ
Innsbruck

SWITZERLAND

dairy cattle
Alps Mts
skiing
snowboardi

Lake Geneva
Red Cross
ITALY

LIECHTENSTEIN

Matterhorn

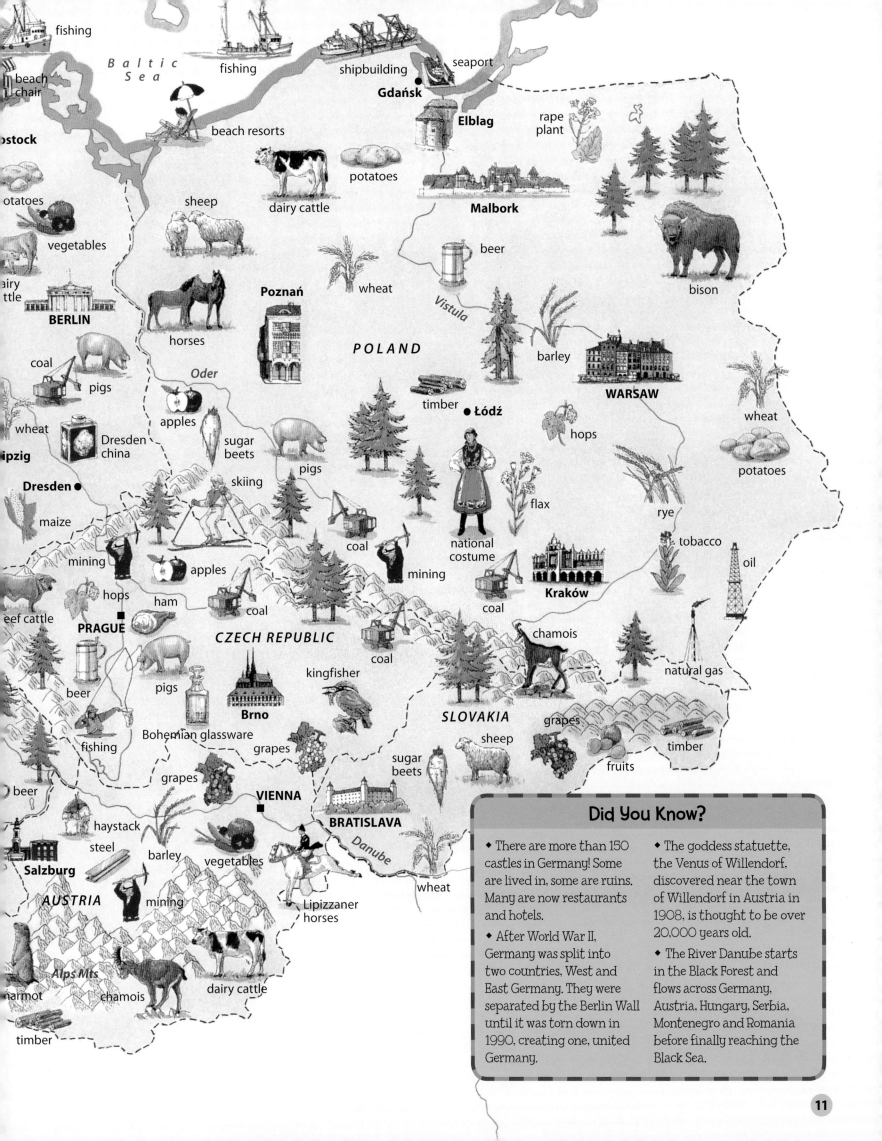

fishing

B a l t i c
S e a

beach
chair

fishing

shipbuilding

seaport

Gdańsk

rape
plant

ostock

beach resorts

Elblag

potatoes

dairy cattle

sheep

Malbork

beer

potatoes

vegetables

horses

Poznań

wheat

Vistula

bison

airy
ttle

BERLIN

coal

pigs

Oder

POLAND

barley

WARSAW

apples

timber

Łódź

hops

wheat

wheat

Dresden
china

sugar
beets

pigs

potatoes

ipzig

skiing

flax

rye

Dresden

maize

coal

mining

national
costume

tobacco

mining

oil

apples

Kraków

hops

ham

coal

coal

chamois

natural gas

eef cattle

PRAGUE

coal

beer

pigs

kingfisher

SLOVAKIA

grapes

beer

Brno

timber

sheep

Bohemian glassware

grapes

sugar
beets

fruits

fishing

grapes

VIENNA

beer

BRATISLAVA

haystack

Danube

steel

barley

vegetables

wheat

Salzburg

AUSTRIA

mining

Lipizzaner
horses

armot

chamois

dairy cattle

Alps Mts

timber

Did You Know?

◆ There are more than 150 castles in Germany! Some are lived in, some are ruins. Many are now restaurants and hotels.

◆ After World War II, Germany was split into two countries, West and East Germany. They were separated by the Berlin Wall until it was torn down in 1990, creating one, united Germany.

◆ The goddess statuette, the Venus of Willendorf, discovered near the town of Willendorf in Austria in 1908, is thought to be over 20,000 years old.

◆ The River Danube starts in the Black Forest and flows across Germany, Austria, Hungary, Serbia, Montenegro and Romania before finally reaching the Black Sea.

Spain, Portugal and Italy

Several mountain ranges cross Spain. The highest mountains are the Pyrenees, between Spain and France, and the Sierra Nevada in the south. Many Spaniards now live and work in the towns, but others still work on the land, growing olives, citrus fruits and grapes. Portugal, on the southwestern edge of the Iberian Peninsula, is a much smaller country. Many Portuguese are fishermen or farmers.

Italy is a long, narrow country, with the Apennine mountains running through its centre. In the north there are factories where cars and textiles are made. In the south farmers grow fruits, such as olives and oranges.

The climate in Spain, Portugal and Italy is mild. The region's beaches are popular holiday destinations for people from all over the world.

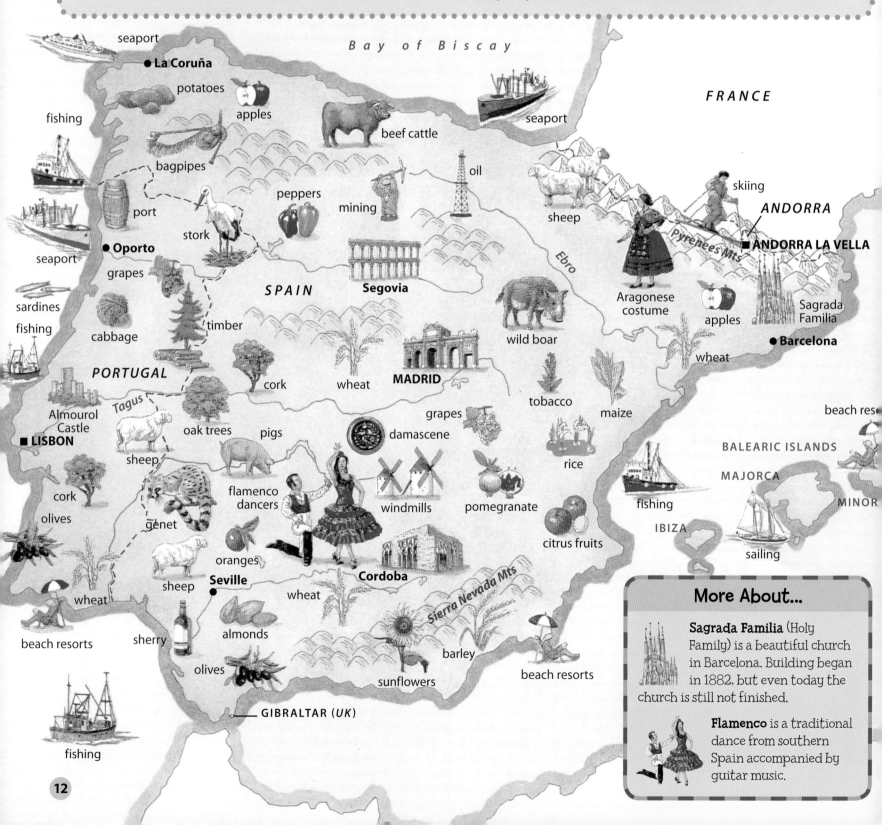

seaport

La Coruña

Bay of Biscay

potatoes

apples

beef cattle

seaport

FRANCE

fishing

bagpipes

oil

skiing

port

peppers

mining

ANDORRA

stork

sheep

Pyrenees Mts

ANDORRA LA VELLA

Oporto

SPAIN

Segovia

Aragonese costume

apples

Sagrada Familia

grapes

seaport

sardines

fishing

cabbage

timber

wild boar

Barcelona

wheat

PORTUGAL

cork

wheat

MADRID

tobacco

maize

Tagus

grapes

beach res

Almourol Castle

oak trees

pigs

damascene

rice

BALEARIC ISLANDS

LISBON

sheep

MAJORCA

MINOR

cork

flamenco dancers

windmills

pomegranate

fishing

olives

genet

IBIZA

oranges

Cordoba

citrus fruits

sailing

sheep

Seville

wheat

Sierra Nevada Mts

wheat

sherry

almonds

barley

beach resorts

beach resorts

olives

sunflowers

GIBRALTAR *(UK)*

fishing

More About...

Sagrada Familia (Holy Family) is a beautiful church in Barcelona. Building began in 1882, but even today the church is still not finished.

Flamenco is a traditional dance from southern Spain accompanied by guitar music.

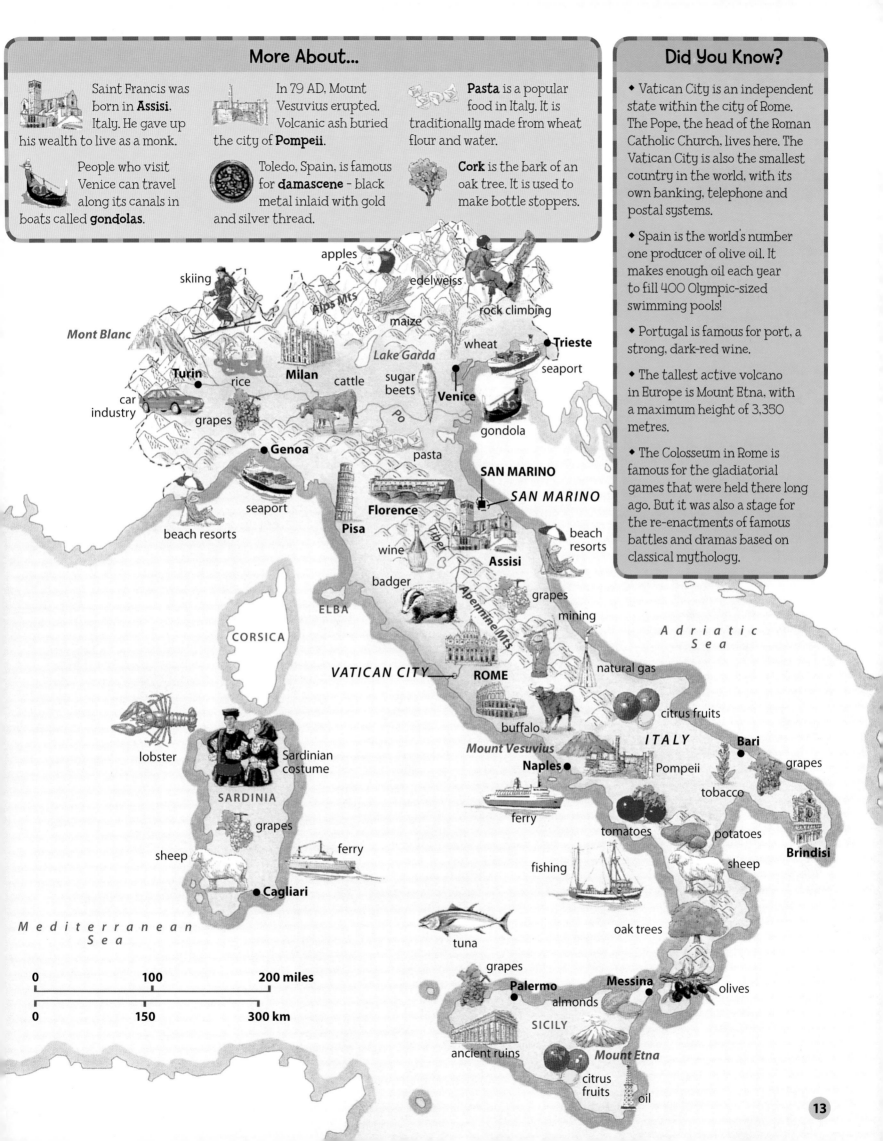

More About...

Saint Francis was born in **Assisi**, Italy. He gave up his wealth to live as a monk.

People who visit Venice can travel along its canals in boats called **gondolas**.

In 79 AD, Mount Vesuvius erupted. Volcanic ash buried the city of **Pompeii**.

Toledo, Spain, is famous for **damascene** - black metal inlaid with gold and silver thread.

Pasta is a popular food in Italy. It is traditionally made from wheat flour and water.

Cork is the bark of an oak tree. It is used to make bottle stoppers.

Did You Know?

◆ Vatican City is an independent state within the city of Rome. The Pope, the head of the Roman Catholic Church, lives here. The Vatican City is also the smallest country in the world, with its own banking, telephone and postal systems.

◆ Spain is the world's number one producer of olive oil. It makes enough oil each year to fill 400 Olympic-sized swimming pools!

◆ Portugal is famous for port, a strong, dark-red wine.

◆ The tallest active volcano in Europe is Mount Etna, with a maximum height of 3,350 metres.

◆ The Colosseum in Rome is famous for the gladiatorial games that were held there long ago. But it was also a stage for the re-enactments of famous battles and dramas based on classical mythology.

apples

skiing

edelweiss

Alps Mts

rock climbing

maize

Mont Blanc

wheat

Trieste

Lake Garda

seaport

Turin

rice

Milan

cattle

sugar beets

Venice

car industry

grapes

Po

gondola

Genoa

pasta

seaport

SAN MARINO

beach resorts

Florence

SAN MARINO

Pisa

wine

beach resorts

badger

Tiber

Assisi

ELBA

grapes

CORSICA

Apennine Mts

mining

Adriatic Sea

natural gas

VATICAN CITY

ROME

lobster

citrus fruits

ITALY

Bari

Sardinian costume

buffalo

grapes

Mount Vesuvius

Naples

Pompeii

SARDINIA

tobacco

grapes

ferry

tomatoes

potatoes

sheep

Brindisi

sheep

fishing

Cagliari

oak trees

M e d i t e r r a n e a n S e a

tuna

grapes

0	100	200 miles

Messina

Palermo

olives

almonds

0	150	300 km

SICILY

ancient ruins

Mount Etna

citrus fruits

oil

13

Southeastern Europe

Hungary, Serbia, Croatia, Romania, Bulgaria and Greece are all part of southeast Europe. Budapest, the capital of Hungary, lies on the banks of the River Danube, which flows south into Serbia – one of the six separate republics that formerly made up the country of Yugoslavia. Differences between the two largest republics, Serbia and Croatia, led to civil war in the 1990s.

The Danube continues its journey to the Black Sea, forming the border between Romania and Bulgaria. Both countries have high mountain ranges: the Carpathians and the Transylvanian Alps in Romania; the Balkans in Bulgaria.

To the south is the mainland of Greece, with its many islands. Tourism is very important to Greece. People come to visit the ancient ruins and to enjoy the country's islands and beaches.

Did You Know?

• The ancient Olympic Games were first held at Olympia, Greece, in 776 BC. The first modern Olympics were held in Athens in 1896.

• Count Dracula, the infamous vampire, is supposed to have come from Transylvania, a region of Romania.

• The Dalmatian coast of Croatia is dotted with many islands. Spotty Dalmatian dogs come from this region.

More About...

 Olives are the fruit of the olive tree. They are green when unripe and turn black as they ripen.

 Pelicans live around the Black Sea. This large bird uses the pouch attached to its bill to scoop up fish from the water for food.

 The beautiful **Samariá Gorge** national park on the Greek island of Crete is a major attraction for tourists.

 Bran Castle was built in 1377 to guard a route over the Transylvanian Alps.

 The Romans built a vast **amphitheatre**, seating thousands of people, at the port of Pula in Croatia.

 The **Golden Kine** (or cows) are part of a gold treasure trove found in Bulgaria. It may be more than 6,000 years old!

 The **Parthenon** temple in Athens, Greece, is more than 2,400 years old. It was built in honour of the Greek goddess of wisdom, Athena.

 The **Valley of Roses** is a rose-growing area in Bulgaria. It also produces a rose oil used in perfumes.

SLOVENI

LJUBLJANA

ZAGF

wolf

coal

Roman amphitheatre

Pula

Dinaric Alps Mts

fishing

Dalmatia

Sp

Adriat Sea

ITALY

0		100		200 miles
0	150		300 km	

olives

Samariá Gorge

beach resort

MALTA ■ **VALLETTA**

UKRAINE

MOLDOVA

timber

coal

grapes

BUDAPEST

Csikós

grapes

HUNGARY

pigs

wheat

sugar beets

rice

lynx

stork

apples

apples

maize

sugar beets

Cluj-Napoca

mining

Carpathian Mts

monastery

grapes

sunflowers

wild boar

natural gas

potatoes

beef cattle

maize

paprika

Drava

Danube

CROATIA

apples

natural gas

dairy cattle

pigs

Transylvanian Alps Mts

skiing

Bran Castle

timber

reeds

pelican

BOSNIA AND HERZEGOVINA

pigs

geese

wheat

BELGRADE

tobacco

ROMANIA

oil

coal

wheat

mining

SARAJEVO

grapes

potatoes

BUCHAREST

grapes

SERBIA

mining

mining

maize

Danube

sugar beets

beach resorts

brown bear

wheat

sunflowers

BULGARIA

wheat

pes

MONTENEGRO

SOFIA

roses

Golden Kine

beach resorts

Dubrovnik

KOSOVO

PRISTINA

coal

Balkan Mts

Black Sea

PODGORICA

timber

grapes

barley

sheep

SKOPJE

tobacco

goat

MACEDONIA

timber

cotton

sheep

cattle

cotton

fishing

TIRANA

Greek dancers

tobacco

ALBANIA

Pindus Mts

LEMNOS

olives

Aegean Sea

CORFU

grapes

Mount Olympus

figs

LESBOS

citrus fruits

sheep

Ionian Sea

KEFALONIA

GREECE

fishing

TURKEY

octopus

olives

The Parthenon

CHIOS

beach resorts

windmills

SAMOS

0   50 miles

Corinth

ATHENS

0   75 km

palm tree

ZAKYNTHOS

seaport

beach resorts

CRETE

mining

NAXOS

ancient ruins

silver

RHODES

15

B e a u f o r t
S e a

QUEEN ELIZABETH ISLAND

snow goose

BANKS
ISLAND

walrus

fur seal

Yukon

Arctic fox

VICTORIA ISLAND

mining

ALASKA
(*USA*)

oil

snowy owl

sea otter

oil

YUKON
TERRITORY

Mackenzie

NORTHWEST
TERRITORIES

Great Bear
Lake

CANADA

moose

Anchorage ●

oil tanker

Inuit

grizzly bear

Whitehorse

harlequin duck

salmon

Yellowknife ●

Great Slave
Lake

oil

P a c i f i c
O c e a n

Rocky Mts

Juneau ●

dolphin

mountain goat

Lake
Athabasca

Did You Know?

♦ Canada has two official
languages: English and French.
Almost a quarter of the people
speak French as their first
language.

♦ Fantastic shimmering
flashes of light often brighten
the Arctic skies in the north
of Canada. They are known
as the aurora borealis, or the
northern lights.

♦ In a museum near the city
of Calgary you can find the
world's largest exhibit of
complete dinosaur skeletons.

salmon

BRITISH COLUMBIA

skiing

pigs

ALBERTA

SASKATCHEWAN

Edmonton ●

VANCOUVER
ISLAND

rodeo

harvesting
wheat

totem
pole

Calgary ●

fishing

Vancouver ●

wheat

seaport

Regina ●

More About...

The **Inuit** people
live in the Arctic.
Some still hunt, but
many now work as
fishermen or miners.

Lumberjacks cut
down trees for
timber in Canada's
forests. It is difficult
and dangerous work.

Until 1929, the **Royal
Canadian Mounted Police
Force** rode on horseback. Today
aircraft and snowmobiles are
often used instead.

The **CN Tower** in Toronto is
553 metres high. When it
opened in 1975 it was the
world's tallest freestanding
structure.

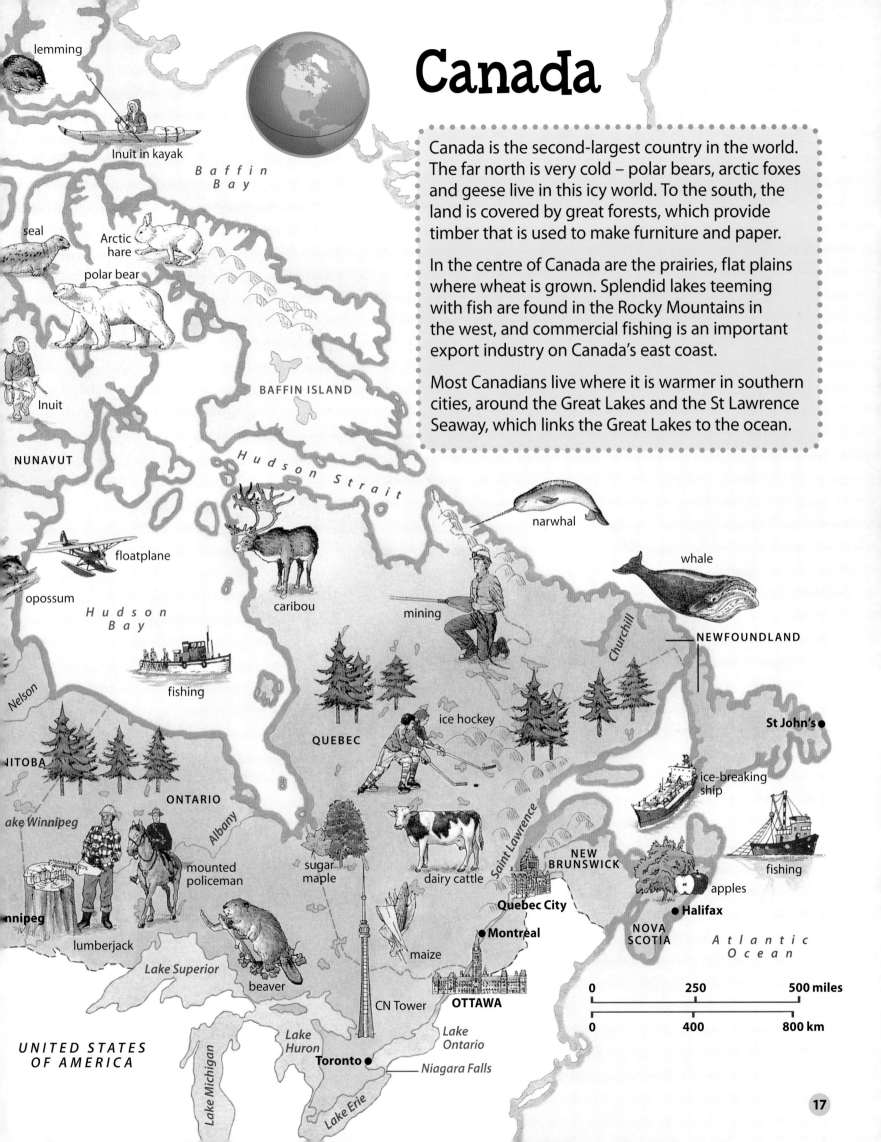

Canada

lemming

Inuit in kayak

Baffin Bay

seal

Arctic hare

polar bear

Inuit

BAFFIN ISLAND

NUNAVUT

Hudson Strait

Canada is the second-largest country in the world. The far north is very cold – polar bears, arctic foxes and geese live in this icy world. To the south, the land is covered by great forests, which provide timber that is used to make furniture and paper.

In the centre of Canada are the prairies, flat plains where wheat is grown. Splendid lakes teeming with fish are found in the Rocky Mountains in the west, and commercial fishing is an important export industry on Canada's east coast.

Most Canadians live where it is warmer in southern cities, around the Great Lakes and the St Lawrence Seaway, which links the Great Lakes to the ocean.

floatplane

opossum

Hudson Bay

caribou

mining

narwhal

whale

Churchill

NEWFOUNDLAND

fishing

Nelson

St John's ●

NITOBA

ice hockey

QUEBEC

ice-breaking ship

ONTARIO

Albany

ake Winnipeg

mounted policeman

sugar maple

dairy cattle

Saint Lawrence

NEW BRUNSWICK

fishing

Quebec City

apples

nnipeg

● Montreal

NOVA SCOTIA

● Halifax

lumberjack

beaver

maize

Atlantic Ocean

Lake Superior

CN Tower

OTTAWA

0	250	500 miles

0	400	800 km

UNITED STATES OF AMERICA

Lake Michigan

Lake Huron

Toronto ●

Lake Ontario

Niagara Falls

Lake Erie

United States of America

The United States of America is made up of 50 states. Forty-eight lie between Canada to the north and Mexico to the south. The 49th and 50th states are separated from the others. Alaska is west of Canada, while Hawaii is made up of islands to the southwest of the mainland, in the Pacific Ocean.

The first people to live in America, the Native Americans, travelled from Asia in prehistoric times. Europeans began to arrive more than 400 years ago. People from all over the world now move to live in the USA.

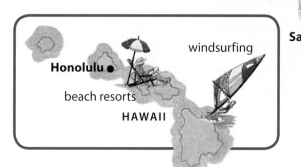

Honolulu
windsurfing
beach resorts
HAWAII

CANADA

apples
Seattle
WASHINGTON
timber
Columbia
Snake
mining
natural gas
grizzly bear
coyo
MONTANA
IDAHO
OREGON
puma
Old Faithful geyser
buff
redwood trees
NEVADA
bald eagle
Rocky Mts
WYOMING
Sierra Nevada Mts
Denv
San Francisco ● **San Jose**
CALIFORNIA
Mojave people
skiing
grapes
UTAH
COLORADO
computer industry
oranges
Las Vegas
Grand Canyon
Los Angeles
Disneyland
San Diego
ARIZONA
Colorado
road runne
Phoenix
NEW MEXICO
mining
saguaro cactus
pueblo

Pacific Ocean

MEXICO

More About...

American **alligators**, once under threat, now live mainly in protected southern swamp areas called the Everglades.

Redwood trees grow in California. Some are more than 2,000 years old. The tallest is 115 metres high.

Huge herds of **buffalo** once roamed the western plains. Today only a few remain.

The **Mojave people** settled in what is now California. Few Native Americans live there today.

The **Old Faithful geyser** in Yellowstone National Park gained its name because it shoots hot water and steam high into the air every hour.

American football teams compete each year to win the prestigious Super Bowl championship game.

RUSSIA

Arctic fox

CANADA

oil

ALASKA

Pacific Ocean

0   250   500 miles

0   400   800 km

beef cattle

pigs

Lake Superior

NORTH DAKOTA

MINNESOTA

MICHIGAN

sugar maple

NEW HAMPSHIRE
VERMONT

MAINE

SOUTH DAKOTA

dairy cattle

Lake Michigan

Lake Huron

car industry

Lake Ontario

NEW YORK

Boston
MASSACHUSETTS

RHODE ISLAND

CONNECTICUT

Mount Rushmore

WISCONSIN

Sears Tower

Detroit

Lake Erie

PENNSYLVANIA

Niagara Falls

Amish farmer

New York

NEW JERSEY

NEBRASKA

harvesting wheat

Chicago

soya beans

steel

Philadelphia

DELAWARE

Baltimore

seaport

prairie dog

IOWA

maize

INDIANA

Columbus

OHIO

coal

WEST VIRGINIA

eep

baseball

Indianapolis

Ohio

WASHINGTON, D.C.

KANSAS

rodeo

ILLINOIS

VIRGINIA

MARYLAND

Missouri

Kansas City

KENTUCKY

NORTH CAROLINA

UNITED STATES OF AMERICA

OKLAHOMA

MISSOURI

American football

Kentucky Derby

TENNESSEE

Appalachian Mts

turkey

tobacco

Atlantic Ocean

beef cattle

cattle ranching

Arkansas

Red

Memphis

Atlanta

SOUTH CAROLINA

fishing

Dallas

ARKANSAS

Mississippi

ALABAMA

cotton

TEXAS

LOUISIANA

Mississippi river boat

peanuts

MISSISSIPPI

GEORGIA

beach resorts

sugarcane

rice

Jacksonville

FLORIDA

Kennedy Space Centre

rattlesnake

San Antonio

oil

Houston

New Orleans

jazz music

seaport

citrus fruits

Rio Grande

brown pelican

fishing

Gulf of Mexico

Miami

alligator

THE BAHAMAS

0   250   500 miles

0   400   800 km

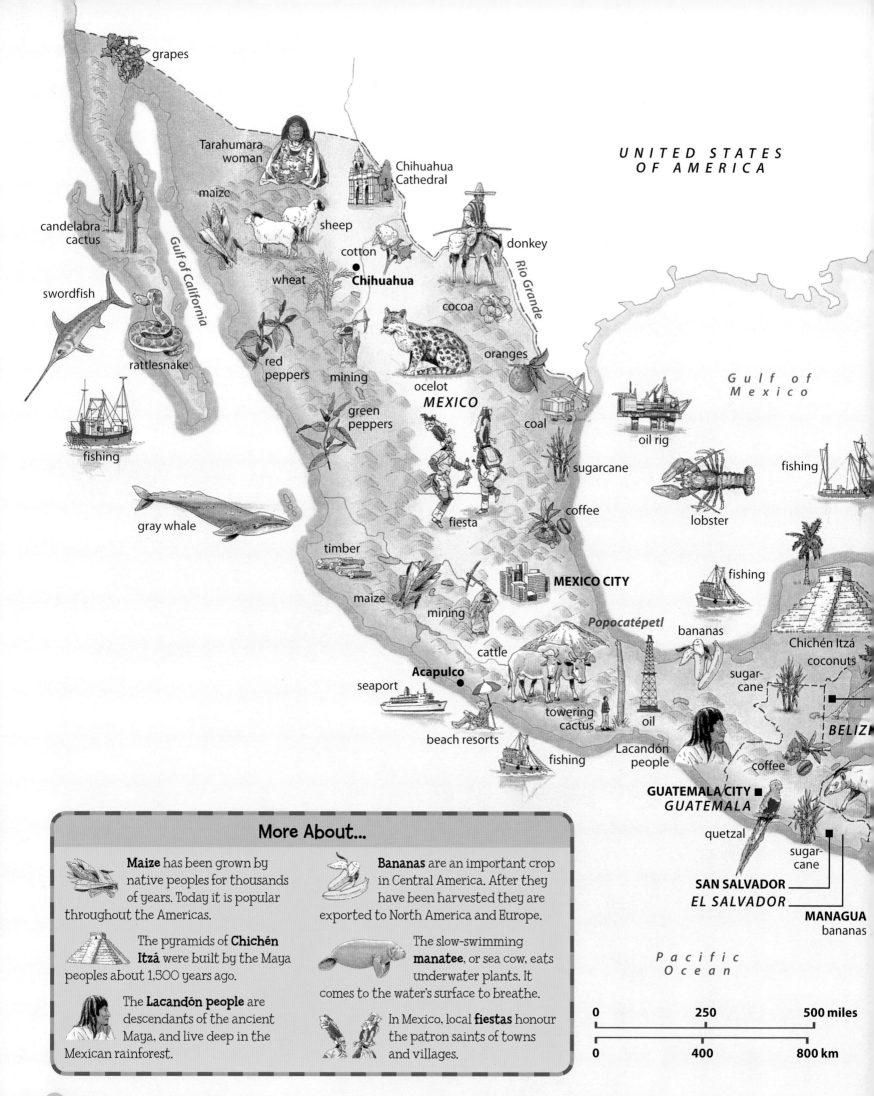

grapes

Tarahumara woman

maize

Chihuahua Cathedral

candelabra cactus

Gulf of California

sheep

cotton

Chihuahua

donkey

Rio Grande

swordfish

rattlesnake

wheat

cocoa

red peppers

mining

oranges

ocelot

MEXICO

green peppers

coal

UNITED STATES OF AMERICA

Gulf of Mexico

oil rig

sugarcane

coffee

fishing

lobster

fishing

gray whale

fiesta

timber

MEXICO CITY

maize

mining

Popocatépetl

bananas

Chichén Itzá

coconuts

cattle

sugar-cane

seaport

Acapulco

towering cactus

oil

BELIZ

beach resorts

fishing

Lacandón people

coffee

GUATEMALA CITY
GUATEMALA

quetzal

sugar-cane

SAN SALVADOR
EL SALVADOR

MANAGUA
bananas

Pacific Ocean

More About...

Maize has been grown by native peoples for thousands of years. Today it is popular throughout the Americas.

The pyramids of **Chichén Itzá** were built by the Maya peoples about 1,500 years ago.

The **Lacandón people** are descendants of the ancient Maya, and live deep in the Mexican rainforest.

Bananas are an important crop in Central America. After they have been harvested they are exported to North America and Europe.

The slow-swimming **manatee**, or sea cow, eats underwater plants. It comes to the water's surface to breathe.

In Mexico, local **fiestas** honour the patron saints of towns and villages.

0	250	500 miles
0	400	800 km

Mexico, Central America and the Caribbean

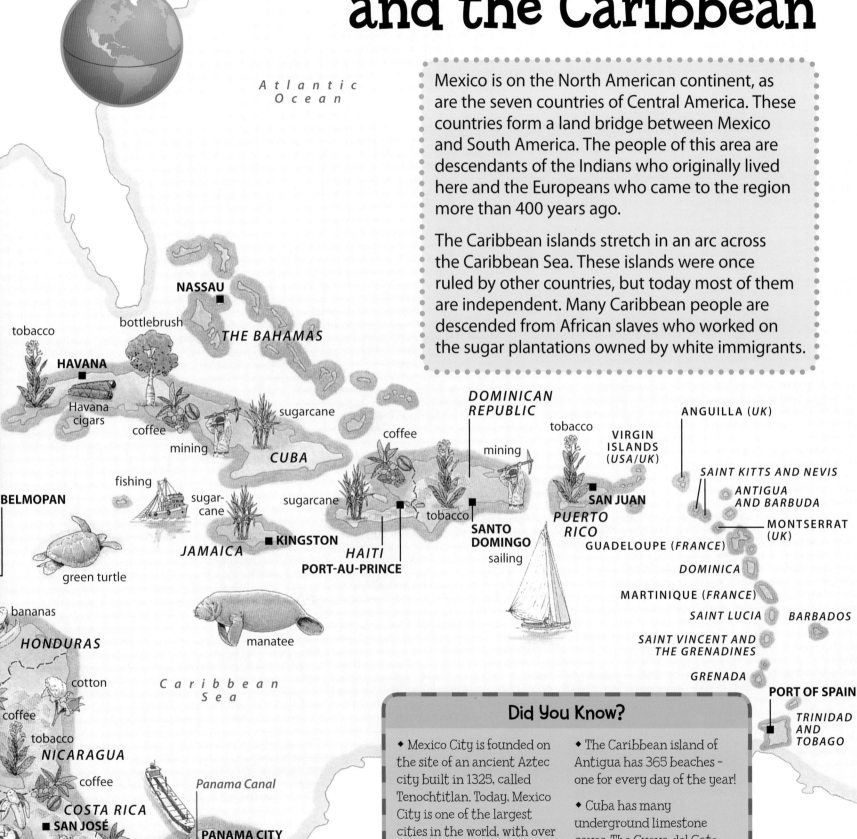

Atlantic Ocean

Mexico is on the North American continent, as are the seven countries of Central America. These countries form a land bridge between Mexico and South America. The people of this area are descendants of the Indians who originally lived here and the Europeans who came to the region more than 400 years ago.

The Caribbean islands stretch in an arc across the Caribbean Sea. These islands were once ruled by other countries, but today most of them are independent. Many Caribbean people are descended from African slaves who worked on the sugar plantations owned by white immigrants.

NASSAU

tobacco

bottlebrush

THE BAHAMAS

HAVANA

Havana cigars

coffee

mining

sugarcane

CUBA

fishing

DOMINICAN REPUBLIC

coffee

mining

tobacco

ANGUILLA (*UK*)

VIRGIN ISLANDS (*USA/UK*)

SAINT KITTS AND NEVIS

ANTIGUA AND BARBUDA

SAN JUAN

PUERTO RICO

MONTSERRAT (UK)

BELMOPAN

sugar-cane

sugarcane

SANTO DOMINGO

GUADELOUPE (*FRANCE*)

green turtle

KINGSTON

JAMAICA

HAITI

PORT-AU-PRINCE

sailing

DOMINICA

MARTINIQUE (*FRANCE*)

bananas

manatee

SAINT LUCIA

BARBADOS

HONDURAS

SAINT VINCENT AND THE GRENADINES

cotton

Caribbean Sea

GRENADA

coffee

tobacco

NICARAGUA

PORT OF SPAIN

TRINIDAD AND TOBAGO

coffee

Panama Canal

COSTA RICA

SAN JOSÉ

PANAMA CITY

PANAMA

timber

cocoa

coffee

toucan

Did You Know?

- Mexico City is founded on the site of an ancient Aztec city built in 1325, called Tenochtitlan. Today, Mexico City is one of the largest cities in the world, with over 21 million people living in Greater Mexico City.

- The name Guatemala means 'land of the trees' in Maya-Toltec language.

- The Caribbean island of Antigua has 365 beaches – one for every day of the year!

- Cuba has many underground limestone caves. The Cueva del Gato Jibaro is 11 kilometres long, and the Cueva Santa Catalina is famous for its giant mushroom-shaped mineral formations!

Northern South America

The landscape of this region varies from the high Andes mountains and desert in the west to thick rainforest in the north and east. The Andes, which run down the west coast of South America, are rich in minerals such as silver, zinc and iron. The Amazon River begins high in the mountains of Peru and flows across Brazil. It is fed by hundreds of small rivers in Peru, Bolivia, Ecuador, Colombia and Venezuela.

Highlands stretch across Venezuela into Guyana, Suriname and French Guiana. The highlands are mainly rainforest, with small areas of grassland. Venezuela is the richest country in the region. It is one of the world's major oil producers.

The first people in South America were American Indians. Today its people are descendants of American Indians and of the Europeans who settled there more than 450 years ago.

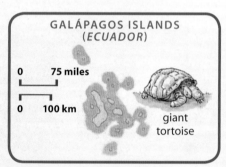

GALÁPAGOS ISLANDS
(*ECUADOR*)

0 75 miles

0 100 km

giant tortoise

More About...

 Giant tortoises live on the Galápagos Islands in the Pacific Ocean. They grow up to 1.5 metres long, can weigh 159 kilograms and live for over 100 years, but today they are an endangered species.

 Panama hats are world famous. They are made from leaves of the palm-like jipijapa plant, which grows in Ecuador.

 The **condor** is a huge bird that is part of the vulture family. It soars high over the Andes and has an enormous wingspan of 3 metres.

 The surviving **Cuiva Indians** live in small groups on the plains of Colombia. Every four weeks they move camp. They hunt wild pigs, catch fish and gather fruit.

 The ruins of the ancient Inca city of **Machu Picchu** were found in 1911. Today it is one of Peru's most popular tourist sites.

 The **Aymara Indians** live high in the Andes mountains. They fish on Lake Titicaca; their boats are made from lakeshore reeds.

 Armadillo means 'little armoured one' in Spanish. It has hard plates covering its back and sides. This burrowing animal curls up in a ball to protect itself when it senses danger.

 Angel Falls, in Venezuela, is the world's highest waterfall, plunging more than 975 metres into the river below.

 Cayenne pepper is bright red and very hot! It is a spice that comes from a plant grown around Cayenne, the capital of French Guiana.

Caribbean Sea

Lake Maracaibo

Atlantic Ocean

natural gas

tobacco

oil

CARACAS

VENEZUELA

oil

TRINIDAD AND TOBAGO

mining

PANAMA

armadillo

cattle

Orinoco

Angel Falls

tobacco

maize

sugarcane

fishing

GEORGETOWN

PARAMARIBO

shrimp

CAYENNE

Gulf of Panama

fishing

BOGOTA

COLOMBIA

Cuiva Indian

coffee

cocoa

Guyana Highlands

diamonds

Guaviare

mining

GUYANA

rice

sugar-cane

FRENCH GUIANA (FRANCE)

Medellín

mining

Cayenne pepper

SURINAME

BRAZIL

Aztec statue

Jupura

potatoes

Barisana Indian

bananas

dines

nama hat

QUITO

ECUADOR Cotopaxi

Guayaquil

Auca Indian

Amazon

eaport

coffee

Marañón

jaguar

macaw

0   300   600 miles

0   400   800 km

cotton

mining

sheep

maize

rubber

sugarcane

PERU

timber

spider monkey

fishing

Machu Picchu

Quechua Indian

sheep

anchovies

LIMA

condor

Aymara Indian

BOLIVIA

oil

llama

Lake Titicaca

LA PAZ

musician

Pacific Ocean

Indian festival

mining

Did You Know?

♦ Cotopaxi, in the Andes of Ecuador, is the highest active volcano in the world. It rises to 5,896 metres above sea level.

♦ Spanish explorers tried to find El Dorado in the Guyana Highlands. Legend said it was a city of gold and great riches.

♦ Spider monkeys are so called because of their very long legs, long tail and small head. They live in South American forests.

♦ Lake Titicaca in the Andes mountains - the largest lake in South America - is fed by 25 rivers. It is also the highest lake in the world on which large boats can sail.

Brazil

Brazil is the largest country in South America, and is home to the biggest tropical rainforest in the world. The River Amazon runs through this hot, steamy rainforest region. Some Indian tribes still live here. The main cities are in the south of the country. São Paulo is the largest city. Rio de Janeiro, famed for its beaches, is known for its annual carnival. In 1960, the newly built city of Brasília became Brazil's capital.

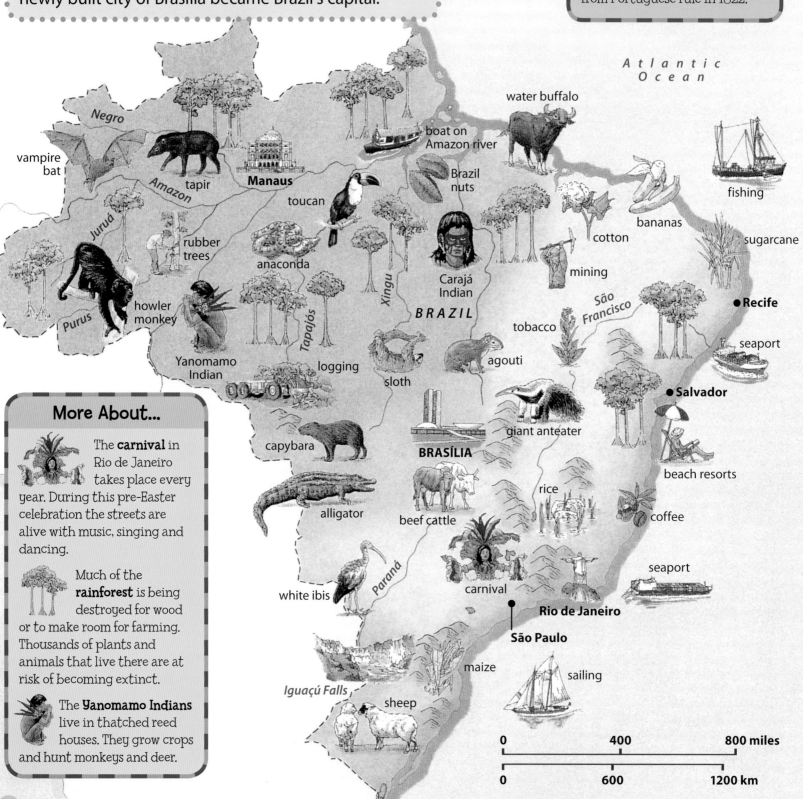

Atlantic Ocean

Negro

water buffalo

vampire bat

Amazon

tapir

Jurua

Manaus

boat on Amazon river

Brazil nuts

fishing

toucan

rubber trees

anaconda

Purus

howler monkey

Xingu

Carajá Indian

B R A Z I L

bananas

cotton

sugarcane

mining

São Francisco

●**Recife**

tobacco

seaport

Yanomamo Indian

Tapajós

logging

sloth

agouti

giant anteater

●**Salvador**

capybara

BRASÍLIA

beach resorts

rice

alligator

beef cattle

coffee

white ibis

Paraná

carnival

seaport

Iguaçú Falls

maize

sailing

Rio de Janeiro

São Paulo

sheep

More About...

The **carnival** in Rio de Janeiro takes place every year. During this pre-Easter celebration the streets are alive with music, singing and dancing.

Much of the **rainforest** is being destroyed for wood or to make room for farming. Thousands of plants and animals that live there are at risk of becoming extinct.

The **Yanomamo Indians** live in thatched reed houses. They grow crops and hunt monkeys and deer.

0	400	800 miles

0	600	1200 km

Southern South America

The Andes mountain range stretches south through Chile and Argentina, as far as the tip of the South American continent. The Andes dominate Chile, which is a long, narrow country on the Pacific coast. To the east are vast areas of grassland in Argentina, Paraguay and Uruguay. Cattle and sheep graze here. Wheat and maize grow on the pampas – flat, treeless plains in Argentina. In the south, there are big reserves of oil and gas. The climate is colder than in the north, and there are many lakes, waterfalls and volcanoes.

As in the rest of South America, the people of these countries are descended mainly from Native Americans and Spanish settlers. Most people live in big cities. The capitals of Argentina, Chile and Uruguay – Buenos Aires, Santiago and Montevideo, respectively – are home to over a third of each country's population.

More About...

The **pricky pear cactus** grows in the deserts of North and South America and produces pear-like fruit covered in thorns.

Gauchos are Argentinian cowboys. They herd cattle on grassy plains called the Pampas.

Football is the national sport throughout South America. Argentina and Uruguay have each won the World Cup twice, but Brazil has won five times.

The **Andes** form the longest mountain chain in the world, stretching for about 7,000 kilometres.

Did You Know?

◆ The Tierra del Fuego islands are shared by two countries. The western islands belong to Chile, and the eastern islands are Argentinian.

◆ Many interesting and unusual animals live in the Andes. Llamas, guanacos, alpacas, and vicuñas are all members of the camel family.

◆ Monkey puzzle trees grow in Chile and Argentina. They got their name because it is said even monkeys find them hard to climb.

◆ It is said that as he died, Jose Artigas, known as the 'father of Uruguan freedom', requested a horse so he could die in the saddle as a gaucho.

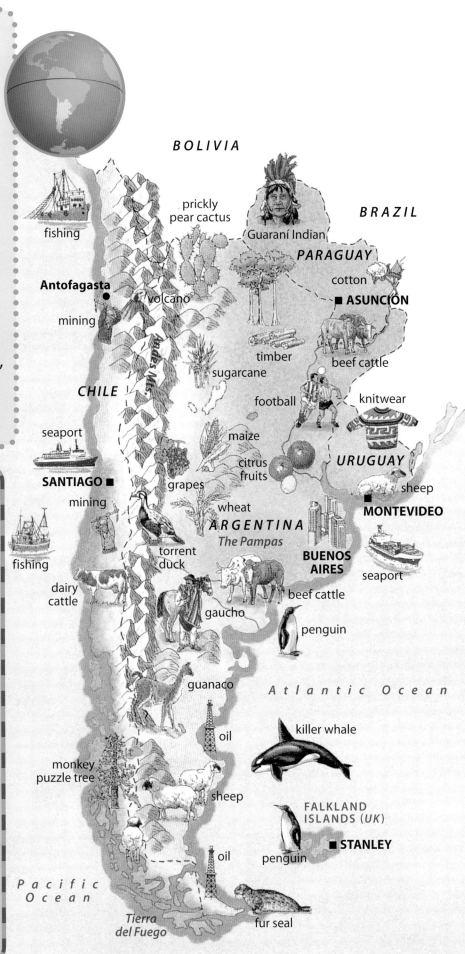

BOLIVIA

BRAZIL

fishing

prickly pear cactus

Guaraní Indian

PARAGUAY

cotton

Antofagasta

volcano

■ **ASUNCIÓN**

mining

timber

beef cattle

sugarcane

CHILE

football

knitwear

seaport

maize

URUGUAY

SANTIAGO ■

grapes

citrus fruits

sheep

mining

wheat

MONTEVIDEO

ARGENTINA
The Pampas

torrent duck

BUENOS AIRES

fishing

dairy cattle

beef cattle

seaport

gaucho

penguin

guanaco

Atlantic Ocean

oil

killer whale

monkey puzzle tree

sheep

FALKLAND ISLANDS (*UK*)

oil

penguin

■ **STANLEY**

Pacific Ocean

Tierra del Fuego

fur seal

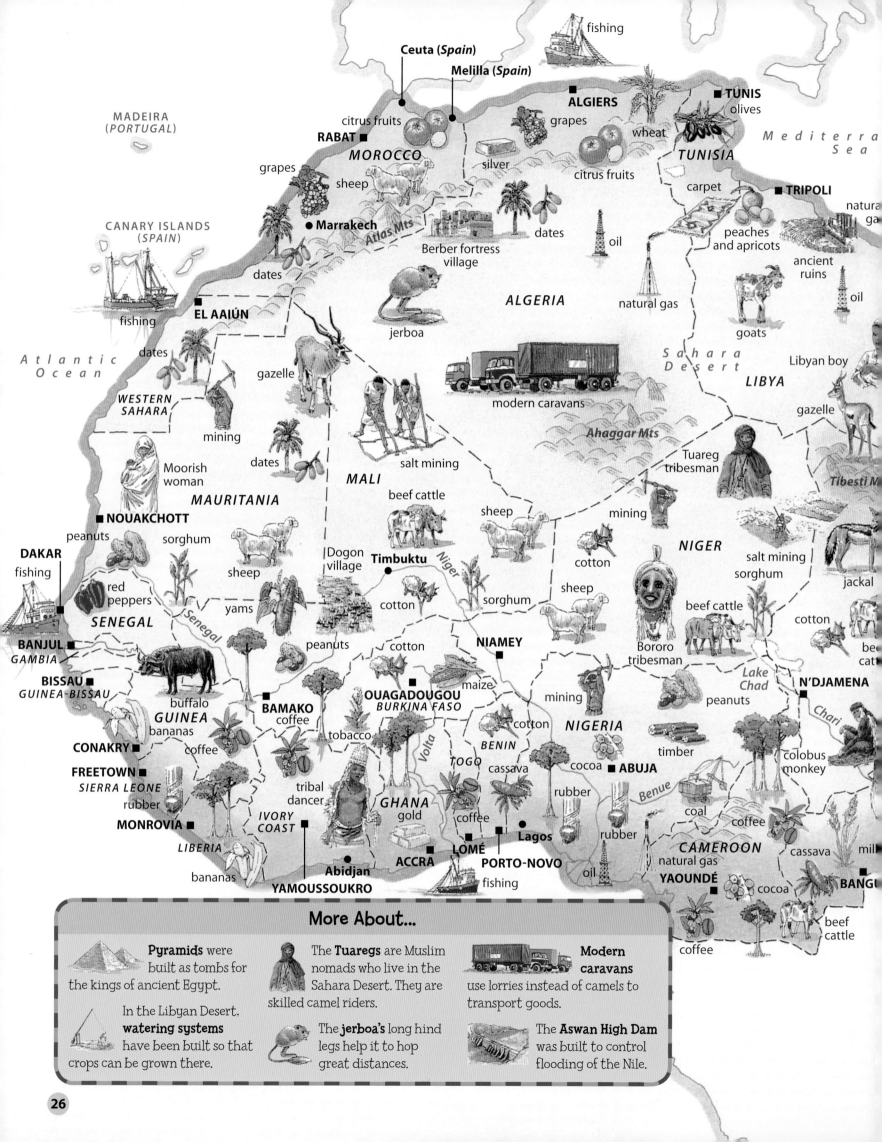

fishing

Ceuta (Spain)

Melilla (Spain)

ALGIERS

TUNIS

olives

Mediterra
Sea

MADEIRA
(PORTUGAL)

citrus fruits

grapes

wheat

RABAT

MOROCCO

silver

TUNISIA

citrus fruits

carpet

TRIPOLI

grapes

sheep

natura
ga

• Marrakech

dates

peaches
and apricots

CANARY ISLANDS
(SPAIN)

Atlas Mts

Berber fortress
village

oil

ancient
ruins

oil

ALGERIA

natural gas

goats

dates

EL AAIÚN

fishing

jerboa

Sahara
Desert

Libyan boy

Atlantic
Ocean

dates

LIBYA

gazelle

WESTERN
SAHARA

gazelle

mining

modern caravans

Ahaggar Mts

Tuareg
tribesman

Tibesti M

dates

salt mining

Moorish
woman

MALI

beef cattle

mining

MAURITANIA

sheep

NIGER

salt mining
sorghum

NOUAKCHOTT

peanuts

sorghum

cotton

jackal

DAKAR

fishing

sheep

Dogon
village

Timbuktu

sheep

cotton

beef cattle

cotton

red
peppers

yams

Niger

cotton

sorghum

Bororo
tribesman

Senegal

SENEGAL

peanuts

cotton

NIAMEY

Lake
Chad

BANJUL
GAMBIA

maize

mining

peanuts

N'DJAMENA

BISSAU
GUINEA-BISSAU

buffalo

OUAGADOUGOU
BURKINA FASO

cotton

NIGERIA

Chari

GUINEA

bananas

BAMAKO
coffee

Volta

BENIN

timber

CONAKRY

coffee

tobacco

TOGO

cocoa

ABUJA

colobus
monkey

FREETOWN
SIERRA LEONE

rubber

tribal
dancer

GHANA
gold

cassava

coffee

rubber

coal

coffee

MONROVIA

IVORY
COAST

LOMÉ

Lagos

rubber

CAMEROON

cassava

mill

LIBERIA

bananas

ACCRA

PORTO-NOVO

oil

natural gas

YAOUNDÉ

BANG

Abidjan

fishing

cocoa

YAMOUSSOUKRO

beef
cattle

coffee

More About...

Pyramids were
built as tombs for
the kings of ancient Egypt.

The **Tuaregs** are Muslim
nomads who live in the
Sahara Desert. They are
skilled camel riders.

**Modern
caravans**
use lorries instead of camels to
transport goods.

In the Libyan Desert,
watering systems
have been built so that
crops can be grown there.

The **jerboa's** long hind
legs help it to hop
great distances.

The **Aswan High Dam**
was built to control
flooding of the Nile.

West and North Africa

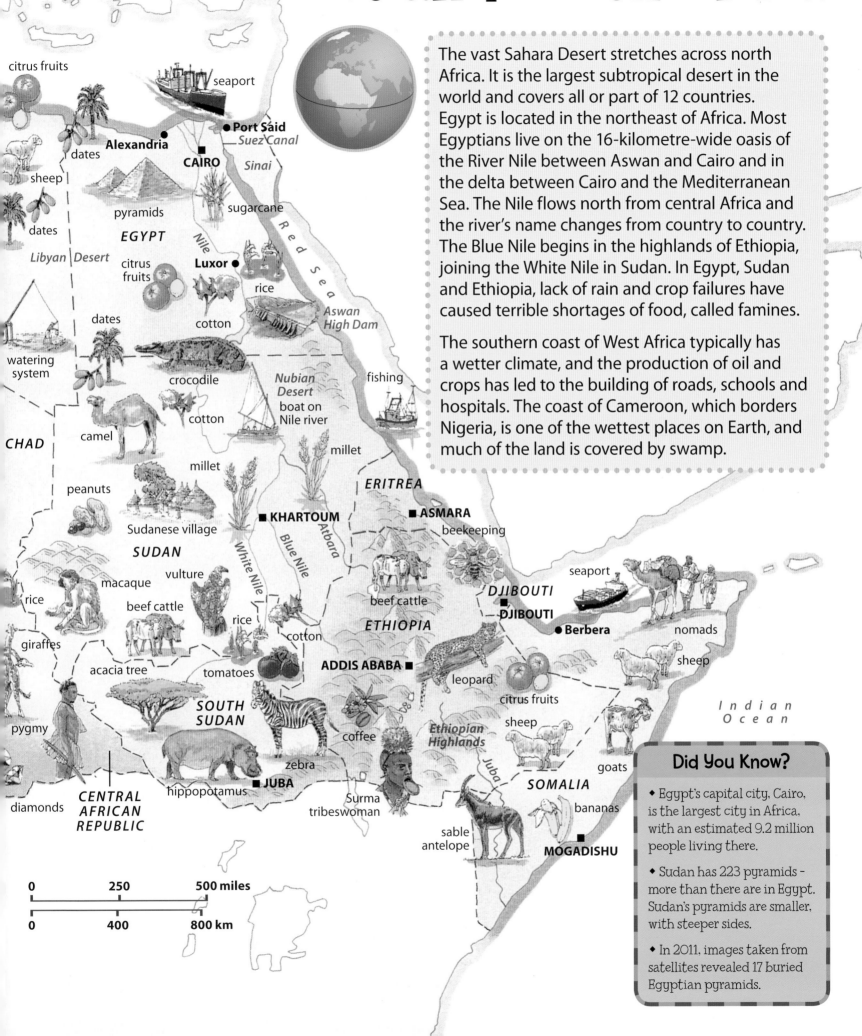

The vast Sahara Desert stretches across north Africa. It is the largest subtropical desert in the world and covers all or part of 12 countries. Egypt is located in the northeast of Africa. Most Egyptians live on the 16-kilometre-wide oasis of the River Nile between Aswan and Cairo and in the delta between Cairo and the Mediterranean Sea. The Nile flows north from central Africa and the river's name changes from country to country. The Blue Nile begins in the highlands of Ethiopia, joining the White Nile in Sudan. In Egypt, Sudan and Ethiopia, lack of rain and crop failures have caused terrible shortages of food, called famines.

The southern coast of West Africa typically has a wetter climate, and the production of oil and crops has led to the building of roads, schools and hospitals. The coast of Cameroon, which borders Nigeria, is one of the wettest places on Earth, and much of the land is covered by swamp.

Map labels

citrus fruits
seaport
dates
Alexandria
● **Port Said**
Suez Canal
sheep
CAIRO
Sinai
pyramids
sugarcane
dates
EGYPT
Nile
Libyan Desert
citrus fruits
Luxor ●
rice
Red Sea
dates
cotton
Aswan High Dam
watering system
crocodile
Nubian Desert
fishing
camel
cotton
boat on Nile river
CHAD
millet
millet
peanuts
ERITREA
KHARTOUM ■
■ **ASMARA**
Sudanese village
beekeeping
SUDAN
seaport
rice
vulture
macaque
beef cattle
White Nile
Blue Nile
Atbara
DJIBOUTI
beef cattle
nomads
giraffes
rice
ETHIOPIA
■ **DJIBOUTI**
sheep
acacia tree
cotton
● **Berbera**
pygmy
tomatoes
ADDIS ABABA ■
leopard
citrus fruits
SOUTH SUDAN
coffee
sheep
Ethiopian Highlands
diamonds
zebra
goats
CENTRAL AFRICAN REPUBLIC
hippopotamus
■ **JUBA**
Surma tribeswoman
Juba
SOMALIA
bananas
sable antelope
■ **MOGADISHU**
Indian Ocean

0   250   500 miles
0   400   800 km

Did You Know?

◆ Egypt's capital city, Cairo, is the largest city in Africa, with an estimated 9.2 million people living there.

◆ Sudan has 223 pyramids – more than there are in Egypt. Sudan's pyramids are smaller, with steeper sides.

◆ In 2011, images taken from satellites revealed 17 buried Egyptian pyramids.

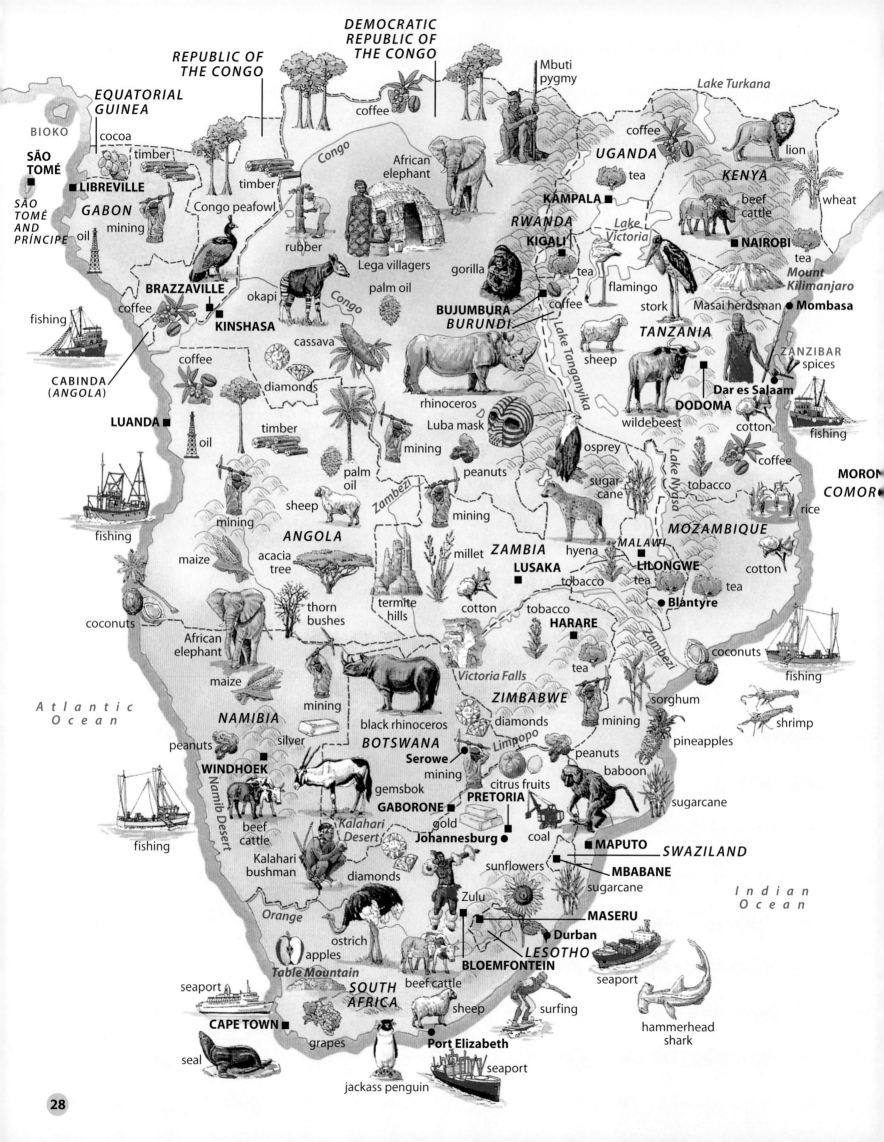

REPUBLIC OF THE CONGO

DEMOCRATIC REPUBLIC OF THE CONGO

EQUATORIAL GUINEA

BIOKO

SÃO TOMÉ

SÃO TOMÉ AND PRÍNCIPE

cocoa

timber

LIBREVILLE

GABON

oil

mining

Congo peafowl

Congo

African elephant

rubber

Lega villagers

BRAZZAVILLE

coffee

okapi

Congo

palm oil

KINSHASA

fishing

CABINDA (ANGOLA)

coffee

diamonds

cassava

LUANDA

oil

timber

palm oil

sheep

mining

fishing

ANGOLA

maize

acacia tree

thorn bushes

termite hills

coconuts

African elephant

maize

mining

NAMIBIA

peanuts

silver

Namib Desert

WINDHOEK

beef cattle

gemsbok

GABORONE

fishing

Kalahari bushman

Kalahari Desert

diamonds

Orange

ostrich

apples

Table Mountain

seaport

CAPE TOWN

seal

grapes

jackass penguin

Mbuti pygmy

Lake Turkana

coffee

UGANDA

tea

KAMPALA

RWANDA

KIGALI

gorilla

tea

coffee

BUJUMBURA

BURUNDI

rhinoceros

Luba mask

mining

peanuts

Zambezi

millet

ZAMBIA

LUSAKA

cotton

mining

hyena

sugar-cane

osprey

Lake Nyasa

tobacco

MALAWI

LILONGWE

tobacco

tea

Blantyre

tobacco

HARARE

ZIMBABWE

Victoria Falls

Zambezi

tea

black rhinoceros

diamonds

mining

BOTSWANA

Serowe

mining

Limpopo

citrus fruits

PRETORIA

gold

coal

Johannesburg

sunflowers

Zulu

BLOEMFONTEIN

beef cattle

sheep

SOUTH AFRICA

surfing

seaport

Port Elizabeth

seaport

hammerhead shark

KENYA

lion

coffee

beef cattle

wheat

NAIROBI

tea

Mount Kilimanjaro

Lake Victoria

flamingo

stork

Masai herdsman

Mombasa

TANZANIA

ZANZIBAR

spices

sheep

DODOMA

Dar es Salaam

wildebeest

cotton

fishing

coffee

MOZAMBIQUE

tobacco

rice

cotton

MORON COMOR

coconuts

fishing

sorghum

shrimp

pineapples

peanuts

baboon

sugarcane

MAPUTO

SWAZILAND

MBABANE

sugarcane

Indian Ocean

MASERU

Durban

LESOTHO

seaport

Atlantic Ocean

Lake Tanganyika

28

South and East Africa

Tropical rainforests are found across the northern part of southern Africa. The Congo river flows through the the Democratic Republic of the Congo on its journey to the Atlantic Ocean. To the east, Kenya and Tanzania are famous for their wildlife. Antelopes, zebras, giraffes, elephants and rhinoceroses live on the savanna, a flat grassland. Snowcapped Mount Kilimanjaro, in Tanzania, is Africa's highest mountain. Farther south are the Kalahari Desert and the smaller Namib Desert.

Most southern African countries are rich in minerals. Zimbabwe has large deposits of copper, iron and gold. In South Africa, coal and the most precious gems – diamonds – are mined.

In 1994 the apartheid system, which had kept the black majority population separate and unequal, was abolished and a new government that was chosen by all the people was put in place.

Madagascar, an island off the east coast of Southern Africa, is home to many unique animal species including the mysterious aye-aye, and lemurs, such as the indri.

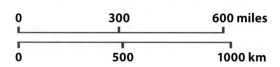

| 0 | 300 | 600 miles |
| 0 | 500 | 1000 km |

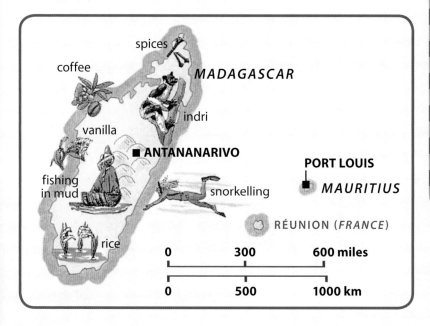

spices
coffee
MADAGASCAR
indri
vanilla
■ ANTANANARIVO
fishing in mud
snorkelling
PORT LOUIS
■ *MAURITIUS*
RÉUNION (*FRANCE*)
rice

| 0 | 300 | 600 miles |
| 0 | 500 | 1000 km |

More About...

 Gorillas live in some African rainforests. They may look fierce, but they are not dangerous unless attacked.

 Miners blast or dig out rocks containing **diamonds**. The gems are then separated from gravel and other rock fragments.

 The **Kalahari bushmen** roam the desert. The women collect roots and berries, while the men hunt.

 Zulus are the largest group of Africans in South Africa. Many now work in the country's cities.

 The spectacular **Victoria Falls**, of the Zambezi River, plunges 108 metres into a giant gorge below.

 The **osprey**, or fish hawk, lives near lakes and rivers. It catches fish with its long claws.

 The tall **Masai** people live on the grasslands of Kenya and Tanzania. They are cattle herders.

 The **rhinoceros** is usually calm, but when it feels threatened it can charge at 50 kilometres per hour.

 Like bees, termites live in groups called colonies. **Termite hills** are the giant nests that termite colonies make from mounds of earth.

 The **Mbuti pygmies** are the smallest people in the world. Their average height is just 1.4 metres.

Post-Soviet States

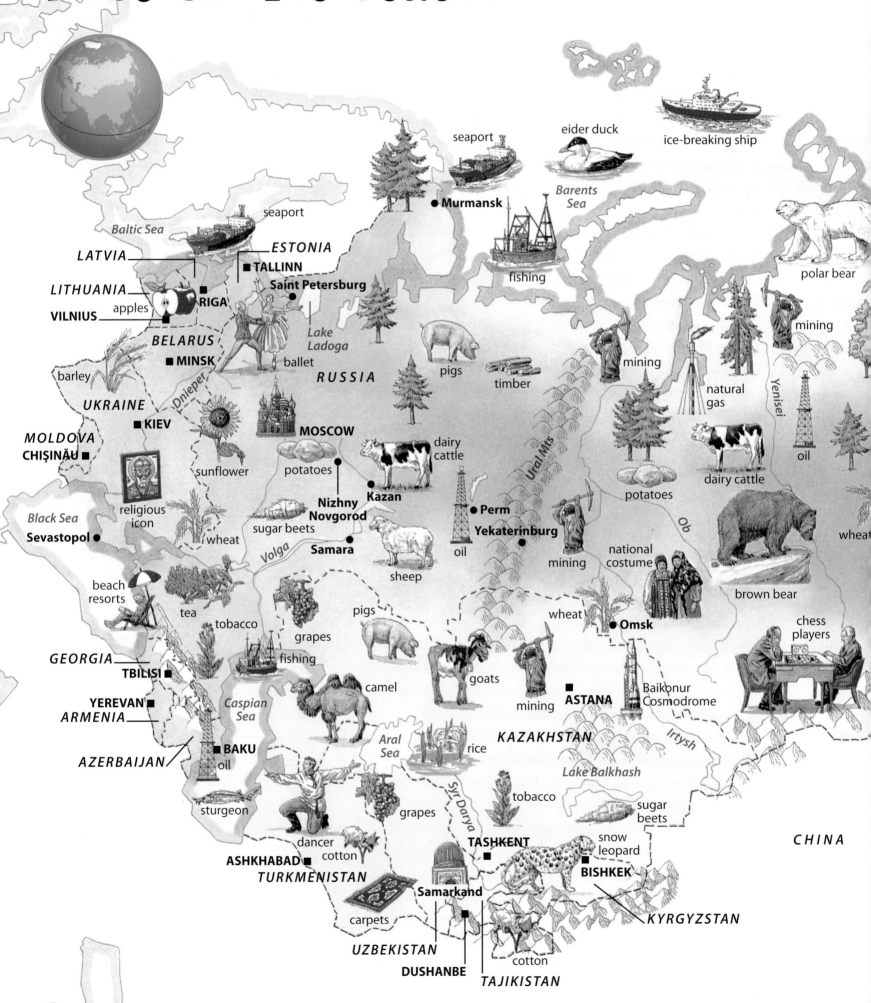

eider duck

ice-breaking ship

seaport

Barents Sea

● Murmansk

fishing

polar bear

Baltic Sea

seaport

LATVIA

ESTONIA

■ TALLINN

LITHUANIA

apples

■ RIGA

Saint Petersburg ●

mining

VILNIUS

Lake Ladoga

BELARUS

ballet

■ MINSK

RUSSIA

pigs

timber

mining

natural gas

Yenisei

barley

UKRAINE

Dnieper

sunflower

potatoes

MOSCOW

dairy cattle

oil

● KIEV

MOLDOVA

dairy cattle

CHIŞINĂU ■

religious icon

sunflower

potatoes

Nizhny Novgorod

Kazan

● Perm

Yekaterinburg

potatoes

Black Sea

wheat

sugar beets

Samara

oil

mining

national costume

brown bear

Sevastopol ●

beach resorts

tea

tobacco

grapes

pigs

sheep

wheat

● Omsk

chess players

GEORGIA

fishing

camel

goats

mining

Baikonur Cosmodrome

TBILISI ■

YEREVAN ■

ARMENIA

Caspian Sea

ASTANA ■

AZERBAIJAN

BAKU

oil

Aral Sea

rice

KAZAKHSTAN

Irtysh

Lake Balkhash

sturgeon

dancer

cotton

grapes

tobacco

sugar beets

CHINA

TASHKENT ■

snow leopard

ASHKHABAD ●

TURKMENISTAN

carpets

Samarkand ■

BISHKEK ●

KYRGYZSTAN

UZBEKISTAN

cotton

DUSHANBE ■

TAJIKISTAN

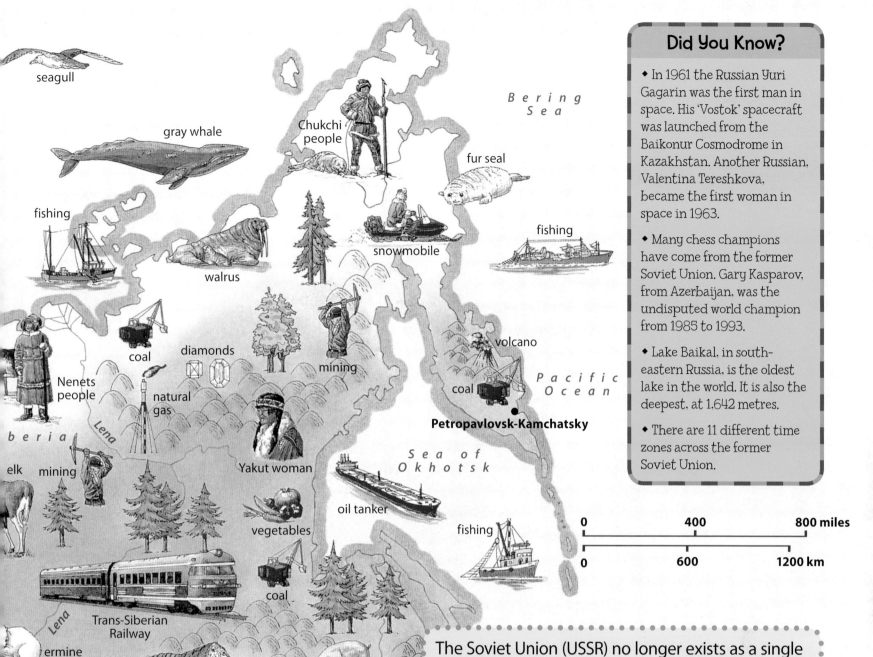

The Soviet Union (USSR) no longer exists as a single country. It was made up of 15 republics, which are now independent countries. Most of these countries form the Commonwealth of Independent States (CIS). Russia is the largest country in the CIS – and also the largest in the world. It stretches from Europe, across the Ural mountains, to northern Asia. In the northeast it is separated from North America by the Bering Strait, a narrow strip of ocean.

The Ural mountains run through Russia from north to south, separating the continents of Europe and Asia. On the European side of the mountains there are more people and industry than on the Asian side. The best land for farming is in the southwest.

Siberia is a vast region, which spreads across Russia from the Ural mountains in the west almost to the Pacific Ocean, and as far north as the Arctic Circle. It is mostly covered in conifer forests, called taiga.

More About...

 The **Trans-Siberian Railway** runs from Moscow to Vladivostok. The journey takes around 6 days.

In the Arctic Ocean, huge **ice-breaking ships** plough through the frozen seas. Smaller ships can then follow.

 The ancient **Nenets people** are reindeer herders. They live in the north of Russia, near the Arctic.

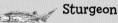 **Sturgeon** can grow to a length of over 5 metres. Their eggs are made into a very expensive food called caviar.

Black Sea

Istanbul

mining

tea

ibex

Lake Urmia

tobacco

Caspian Sea

ANKARA ■

sheep

goatherd

Lake Van

sturgeon

TURKEY

rock dwellings

carpets

İzmir ●

rice

oil

oil

tea

TEHRAN

fac

figs

cotton

grapes

wheat

melons

carpets

Antalya ●

tobacco

sugarcane

cotton

tobacco

Kurdish people

factory

cedar tree

SYRIA

NICOSIA

CYPRUS

BEIRUT ■

BAGHDAD

Isfahan ●

Mediterranean Sea

LEBANON

goats

IRAQ

date palms

fishing

DAMASCUS

ISRAEL

figs

date palms

oil

olives

JERUSALEM ● ■ AMMAN

sheep

WEST BANK
GAZA STRIP
(PALESTINIAN
TERRITORIES)

Ur

reed hut

oil KUWAIT

maize

■ KUWAIT CITY

JORDAN

wheat

natural gas

citrus fruits

Bedouin tent

oil

Persian Gulf

EGYPT

MANAMA

Dammam

BAHRAIN

Arabian horse

falconry

DOHA

QATAR

Arabian Desert

■ RIYADH

SAUDI ARABIA

Red Sea

fennec fox

Medina

camel

Saudi Arabian man

Jeddah ●

● Mecca

jerboa

sand dunes

Empty Quarter

date palms

date palms

grapes

shepherd

wheat

coffee

SANA'A

cotton

YEMEN

factory

wheat

cit

seaport

● Aden

Middle East

The Middle East covers a large area of southwest Asia and northeast Africa. The region is called the 'cradle of civilization' because many ancient civilizations began here. Three world religions also started here – Judaism, Christianity and Islam. Most people in the Middle East are Muslims, followers of Islam. There are Christians and Jews, too. Most Israelis practise Judaism. The ancient Holy Land of Palestine, which is sacred to people of all three religions, falls within Israel and Jordan.

The vast Arabian Desert covers parts of Saudi Arabia, Jordan, Oman, Yemen and the United Arab Emirates. The discovery of oil beneath the desert and in the Persian Gulf has made the countries around the gulf rich.

Throughout history, religious differences and disputes over land and resources have led to many wars in the Middle East, and some conflicts continue to this day.

sheep

Iranian woman

RAN

The Royal Mosque

goat

wild ass

ancient ruins

date palms

il tanker

OMAN

● Dubai — *UNITED ARAB EMIRATES*

oil

oil

ABU DHABI ■

oil

■ **MUSCAT**

manatee

natural gas

date palms

A r a b i a n S e a

orpion

OMAN

Arabian oryx

fishing

tobacco

grapes

0	200	400 miles

0	300	600 km

SOCOTRA

More About...

Bedouins are nomadic tribes who live in the Arabian Desert. They live in tents that they move from place to place.

Saudi Arabia has the world's largest reserves of **oil**. The oil is pumped from the ground and into ships called tankers, which transport it to other countries.

The ruins of **Ur** are in southern Iraq. Ur was one of the most important cities of the ancient Sumerian civilization in Mesopotamia.

A **sand dune** is a ridge of sand formed by the desert wind. Dunes change size and shape as the direction and strength of the wind changes.

Kurds live in the mountainous region where Turkey, Iran and Iraq meet.

Falconry is a traditional form of hunting in Saudi Arabia. Falcons are birds of prey. In the wild they hunt and eat small animals, but in captivity, they are trained to hunt only on command.

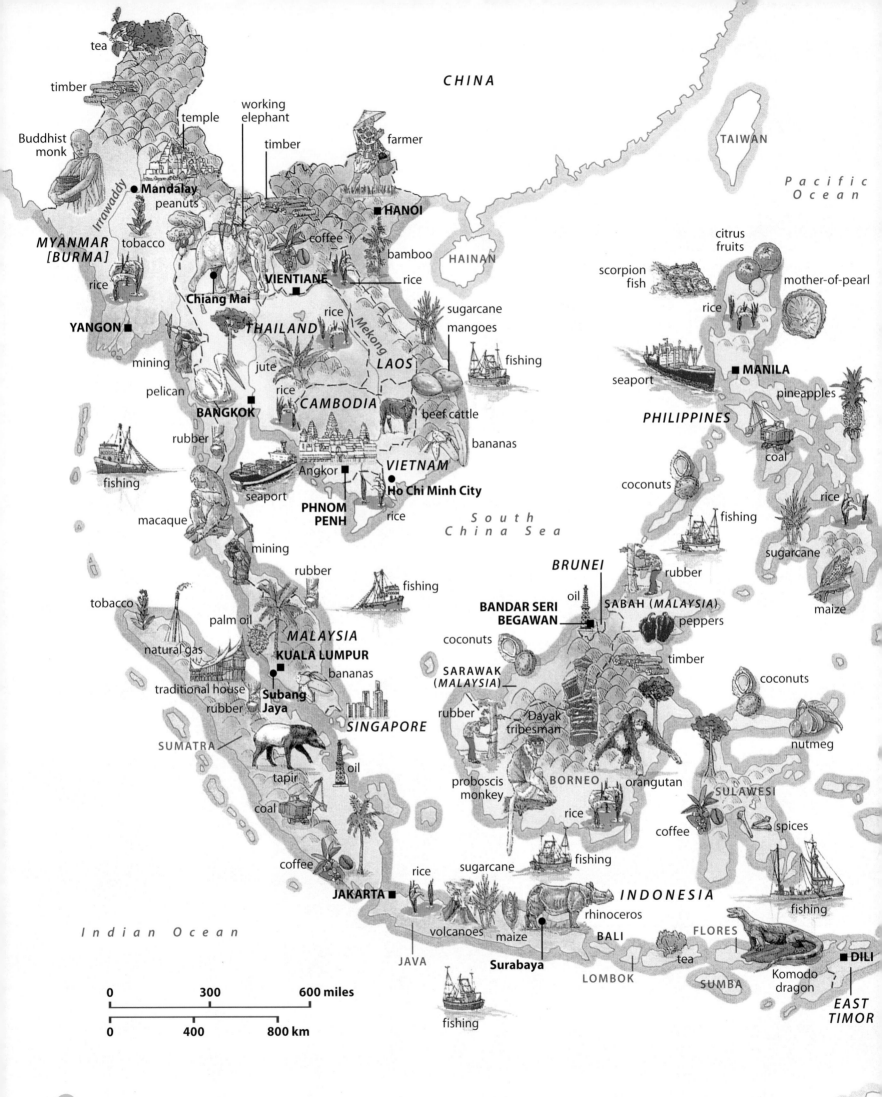

tea

timber

temple

working elephant

timber

CHINA

farmer

TAIWAN

Buddhist monk

Mandalay
peanuts

HANOI

Pacific Ocean

coffee

MYANMAR [BURMA]

tobacco

VIENTIANE

bamboo

HAINAN

rice

citrus fruits

scorpion fish

mother-of-pearl

rice

Chiang Mai

rice

YANGON

THAILAND

sugarcane

mangoes

LAOS

fishing

seaport

MANILA

mining

jute

rice

CAMBODIA

beef cattle

PHILIPPINES

pineapples

pelican

BANGKOK

rubber

Angkor

bananas

coal

fishing

seaport

VIETNAM

South China Sea

coconuts

rice

macaque

PHNOM PENH

Ho Chi Minh City

rice

sugarcane

mining

rubber

fishing

BRUNEI

rubber

maize

tobacco

palm oil

natural gas

MALAYSIA

KUALA LUMPUR

bananas

BANDAR SERI BEGAWAN

oil

SABAH (MALAYSIA)

peppers

coconuts

timber

coconuts

traditional house

rubber

Subang Jaya

SINGAPORE

SARAWAK (MALAYSIA)

rubber

Dayak tribesman

nutmeg

SUMATRA

tapir

oil

proboscis monkey

orangutan

SULAWESI

coal

BORNEO

rice

coffee

spices

coffee

rice

sugarcane

fishing

INDONESIA

fishing

JAKARTA

rhinoceros

FLORES

Indian Ocean

volcanoes

maize

BALI

tea

Komodo dragon

DILI

JAVA

Surabaya

LOMBOK

SUMBA

EAST TIMOR

0   300   600 miles

0   400   800 km

fishing

Southeast Asia

Southeast Asia is made up of more than 20,000 islands. Most of these belong to Indonesia and the Philippines. Indonesia's islands are scattered between the Asian mainland and the northern tip of Australia.

Whilst some countries in Southeast Asia remain relatively less developed, others, including Singapore, Malaysia and Brunei, have used industry, and mineral and oil wealth to develop rapidly into successful economies.

Much of Southeast Asia is covered by lush tropical rainforest, and many of the people are farmers who live near the coast and in river valleys. Indonesia, Thailand, Vietnam and Myanmar – also known as Burma – are among the world's biggest rice producers. Malaysia, Indonesia and Thailand are the world's leading producers of rubber.

More About...

 Most people in **Myanmar** are Buddhists. Between the ages of 6 and 13, boys in Myanmar spend some time as monks, learning to lead a spiritual life.

 Rice is the region's main crop. In many areas it is grown on terraces, which are broad steps cut into the sides of hills or mountains.

 Timber, especially teak, is an important export for some Southeast Asian countries. It is used for furniture and in shipbuilding.

 Volcanic soil from **volcanoes** on the Indonesian island of Java is very fertile, and is good for growing crops.

 The largest lizard in the world is the **Komodo dragon**, which lives on the Lesser Sunda Islands of Indonesia. It can grow to over 3 metres long and has a deadly bite.

 Rubber is made from latex, a milky gum collected from the **rubber tree**. This tree grows in many parts of southeast Asia.

 In Papua New Guinea, people believe in spirits. They build special **spirit houses** to lure any spirits away from their homes.

The island country of **Singapore** is made up of one large city. As well as being a thriving business centre, it is a popular tourist destination and has a busy international port.

Did You Know?

♦ The world's largest producer of tin is Indonesia. This useful metal is also mined in Thailand and Malaysia.

♦ The temples at Angkor in Cambodia were built between the 9th and 12th centuries. Their walls are covered in hand-carved pictures that show historical and religious stories from the ancient Khmer Empire.

♦ Violent tropical storms, called typhoons, are common in the Philippines.

♦ In the forests of Thailand elephants are sometimes still used to move felled teak trees, but are more often used to give rides to tourists.

Pacific Ocean

oil

palm oil

palm trees

rice

WEST PAPUA

palm trees

INDONESIA

NEW GUINEA

PAPUA

Jalé tribesman

PAPUA NEW GUINEA

spirit house

coconuts

palm trees

Puka Puka tribesman

cocoa

bird-of-paradise

PORT MORESBY

fishing

canoe

coconuts

AUSTRALIA

South Asia

To the north of India rise the snow-covered peaks of the Himalaya mountains. The kingdoms of Bhutan and Nepal can be found there. While few people live in the mountains, the plains of India, Pakistan and Bangladesh are more densely populated. The Indian cities of Mumbai, Delhi, Bangalore and Kolkata are home to millions of people. The flat central plains get very dry during the hot season. The rains, when they come, usually last from June to October.

In Bangladesh, most people are farmers, but their crops are often destroyed by floods. Despite this, Bangladesh is a major producer of jute, rice and tropical fruit. Many workers are also employed in the clothing industry.

The Hindu and Buddhist religions started in South Asia. Today India has large numbers of Hindus, while Pakistan and Bangladesh are mainly Muslim.

RUSSIA

natural g

AFGHANISTAN

carpets

shepherd

pomegranates

Kandahar ●

nat

wheat

cotton

pol

IRAN

PAKISTAN

sheep

rice

Karachi

A r a b i a n S e a

Did You Know?

• Tigers once roamed freely in India's forests, but they are now endangered because they have been hunted for their skin and the forests where they live are being cut down. The tigers that remain are protected by law.

• Varanasi is an Indian holy city visited by many pilgrims from different religious faiths. People come from all over South Asia to bathe in the Ganges river. Hindus believe the river is sacred and will purify them.

• The mongoose is a fierce little animal. It eats frogs, birds, lizards and their eggs. Mongooses throw the eggs against stones to break their shells. The Indian grey mongoose can even kill a cobra.

• In 1947, India gained freedom from British rule and was divided into two independent countries, India and Pakistan.

• Together, Sri Lanka and India make South Asia the world's largest producer of tea. Telecommunications, tourism, textiles, chemicals and steel production are all important to India's economy.

• Sherpas are a farming people in Nepal, but they often work as guides for climbers in the Himalaya mountains. In 1953, Sherpa Tenzing Norgay climbed to the top of Mount Everest with the New Zealand explorer Edmund Hillary. This is the earliest record of anyone reaching the summit of the world's highest mountain.

More About...

 Making Afghan **carpets** is a traditional craft. The carpets are made from goat and sheep wool. The wool is dyed and spun, then it is woven on looms.

 Mount Everest lies in the Himalaya mountains. It stands on the border between Nepal and Tibet. At 8,848 metres tall, it is the world's highest mountain.

 Hindus believe that **cows** are sacred, so they never kill or eat them. Cows wander freely in city streets.

 Most **tea** comes from the leaves of a small plant that is widely grown in India and Sri Lanka. The leaves are picked and dried, then sold, either loose or in teabags.

 Polo is a sport that has been played in Pakistan for centuries. Two teams of players on horseback try to hit the ball into the goal using long-handled mallets.

 Taj Mahal means 'crown of the palace'. It was built by Emperor Shah Jahan in memory of his wife.

gazelle

KABUL *Khyber Pass*

snow leopard

Nepalese man with yaks

CHINA

ISLAMABAD

tobacco

coal

carpets sugarcane

Lahore

Amritsar

Faisalabad

tobacco

Indus

cotton

wheat

Thar Desert

nb

derabad

Red Fort

NEW DELHI

Jaipur

Agra

camels

Lucknow

Ganges

Taj Mahal

Varanasi

KATHMANDU

NEPAL

Himalaya Mts

Mount Everest

red panda

timber

tea

BHUTAN

THIMPHU

oil

Brahmaputra

wheat

jute

rice

DHAKA

tobacco

MYANMAR [BURMA]

rhinoceros

rice

steel

DHAKA

cotton

wheat

peanuts

sheep

mongoose

cobra

INDIA

forest

tiger

coal

Kolkata

BANGLADESH

seaport

industry

millet

rice

Mumbai

Godavari

working elephant

seaport

film studios

Hyderabad

Indian hornbill

Bay of Bengal

fishing

Khrishna

cattle

tea

industry

fishing

Western Ghats Mts

peppercorns

Bangalore

Chennai

seaport

coconuts

sacred cow

Indian Ocean

humpback whale

Kochi

tea

coconuts

monkey

SRI LANKA

COLOMBO

0   200   400 miles

0   300   600 km

37

China and Mongolia

Although China is only a little larger than the continental USA it has more than four times as many people. Much of China is so mountainous or dry that few people can live in those areas. Over half the population lives in cities along the coast, on the plains and along China's great rivers. The soil around the Huang He – the Yellow River – is ideal for farming, but most people in China work in factories.

The capital of China, Beijing, is home to more than 19 million people. Shanghai, the largest city and a centre for shipping and industry, has even more inhabitants.

The island of Taiwan lies off the southeast coast of mainland China. North of China is the land-locked independent country of Mongolia. Much of the land is covered by the Gobi Desert, rolling grasslands, or mountains. The Mongolians are expert horsemen who follow their herds of sheep across the plains.

Uygur woman

oil

apples and pears

Tarim

mining

wild ass

melo

Taklimakan Desert

goats

grapes

wheat

potatoes

barley

Tibetan Sherpa

snow leopard

yaks

Himalaya Mts

TIBET

Mount Everest

Lhasa

Potala Palace

More About...

 The **yak** is a type of ox that lives in the Himalaya mountains. Yaks have shaggy hair and long horns. In Tibet, yak milk is used to make sour butter, which is traditionally served in tea.

 The **Great Wall of China** is around 8,850 kilometres long, and was first built to defend the country's northern frontier. From around 200 BC until the 16th century, many sections of the wall were built and rebuilt by different ruling dynasties.

 Bamboo is the largest of the grasses, growing as tall as some trees. Bamboo is eaten by the giant pandas that live in China's bamboo forests.

Set high on a hill, the **Potala Palace** towers above the city of Lhasa in Tibet. Now a museum, it has 1,000 rooms and is a popular tourist attraction. Lhasa is holy to Tibetan Buddhists.

 The two-humped **Bactrian camels** are found in the deserts of China and Mongolia. Their thick fur and stocky bodies help them survive the cold winters. Unfortunately, they are almost extinct in the wild.

 Many Mongolians live in round tents made of felt, which they call **gers**. They tie their gers onto the backs of camels when they travel to a new place.

Did You Know?

♦ In China, each year is named after one of 12 animals: the rat, ox, tiger, rabbit, dragon, snake, horse, ram, monkey, rooster, dog or pig.

♦ More people live in China than any other country. About one fifth of the world's population live there.

♦ Hong Kong, with its magnificent harbour, is a leading port and commerical centre.

♦ The Mongol Empire was once the largest in the world. A 40-metre-high statue of its founder, Genghis Khan, stands to the east of the capital, Ulan Bator.

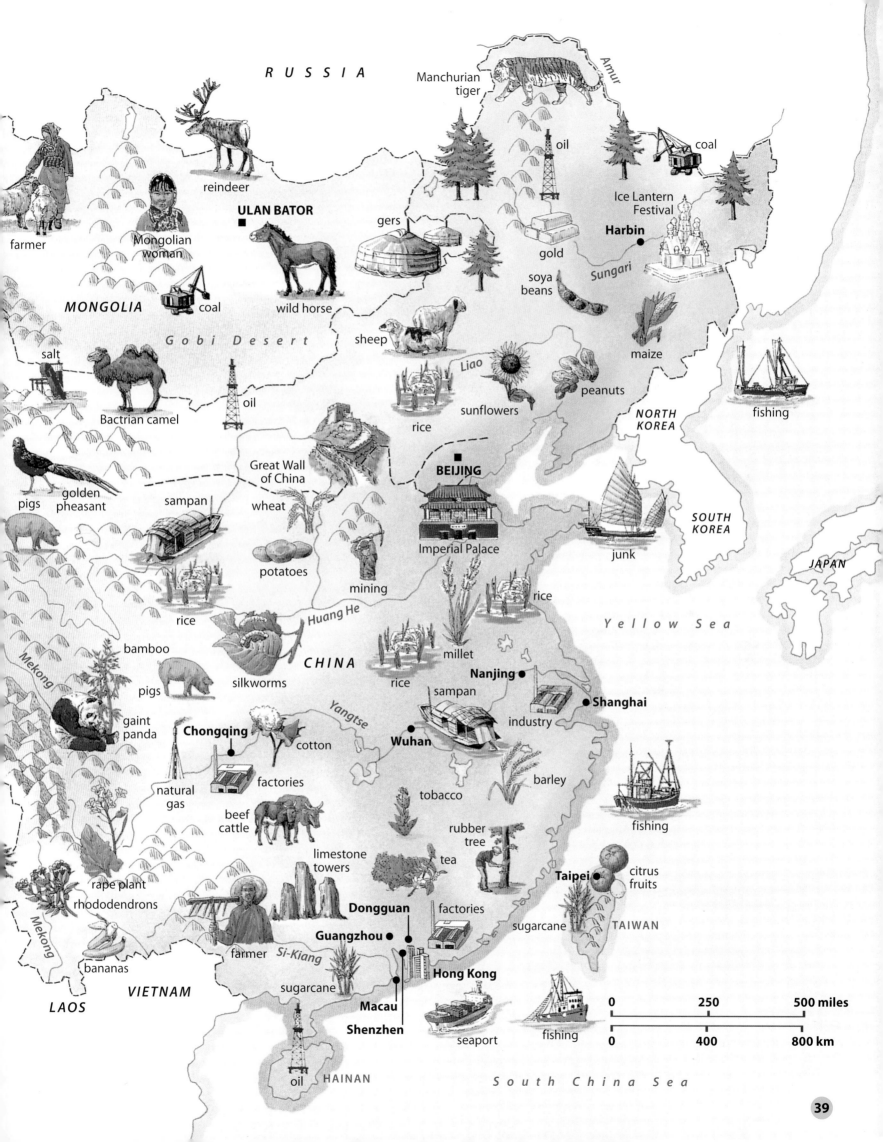

RUSSIA

Manchurian tiger

Amur

oil

coal

reindeer

Ice Lantern Festival

ULAN BATOR

gers

Harbin

gold

farmer

soya beans

Sungari

Mongolian woman

MONGOLIA

coal

wild horse

maize

Gobi Desert

salt

sheep

Liao

fishing

oil

sunflowers

peanuts

NORTH KOREA

Bactrian camel

rice

Great Wall of China

wheat

BEIJING

SOUTH KOREA

golden pheasant

pigs

sampan

junk

JAPAN

potatoes

Imperial Palace

mining

rice

rice

Huang He

CHINA

millet

Yellow Sea

bamboo

silkworms

rice

Nanjing

Mekong

pigs

Yangtse

sampan

Shanghai

gaint panda

Chongqing

cotton

Wuhan

industry

natural gas

factories

barley

beef cattle

tobacco

limestone towers

rubber tree

fishing

rape plant

tea

rhododendrons

Dongguan

Taipei

citrus fruits

factories

Mekong

farmer

Si-Kiang

Guangzhou

sugarcane

TAIWAN

bananas

Hong Kong

LAOS

VIETNAM

sugarcane

Macau

Shenzhen

seaport

fishing

oil

HAINAN

South China Sea

0   250   500 miles

0   400   800 km

Japan and Korea

Japan consists of four main islands. Hokkaidō, Honshū, Shikoku and Kyūshū. There are more than 3,000 smaller islands, but most of these are uninhabited. A chain of volcanic mountains runs across Japan, and there are frequent earthquakes.

The southern islands are hot and damp, while the northen islands are colder. Mountains and forests cover much of the land. Rice is the main crop. Fishing is also important. Japan is one of the world's leading makers of ships, cars and electronic equipment. Most Japanese people enjoy a high standard of living.

Korea lies to the west of Japan. In North Korea the winters are very cold, and the climate is suitable for growing potatoes and corn. Mining and industry are important there. South Korea has a warmer climate, which is well suited to farming, but the country also has many factories and its products are exported all over the world.

Did You Know?

• The Japanese pay special attention to nature. In Japanese gardens, rocks, pools and waterfalls are used to create landscapes.

• The cherry blossom is the national flower of Japan. Every spring people come to Ōsaka to see the cherry trees in bloom. People sit in special pavilions to enjoy the beautiful scenery.

• In the early 21st century, over 120 different newspapers were published daily in Japan, selling nearly 72 million copies every day.

• Mount Fuji is a volcano that towers above five beautiful lakes. It last erupted in 1707. Many Japanese believe Mount Fuji is sacred.

• Most of Japan's population live in towns and cities. Twelve Japanese cities each have more than a million people living there.

• In Gifu, in the Chūbu region of Japan, fishermen use cormorants as helpers. The birds are attached to the boats by long ropes. They dive into the water to catch fish, but rings placed around their necks prevent them from swallowing their catch.

• Visitors to a Japanese home are expected to take off their shoes and leave them at the door. Guest slippers are provided for walking in hallways, but must be removed in rooms with straw mats on the floor.

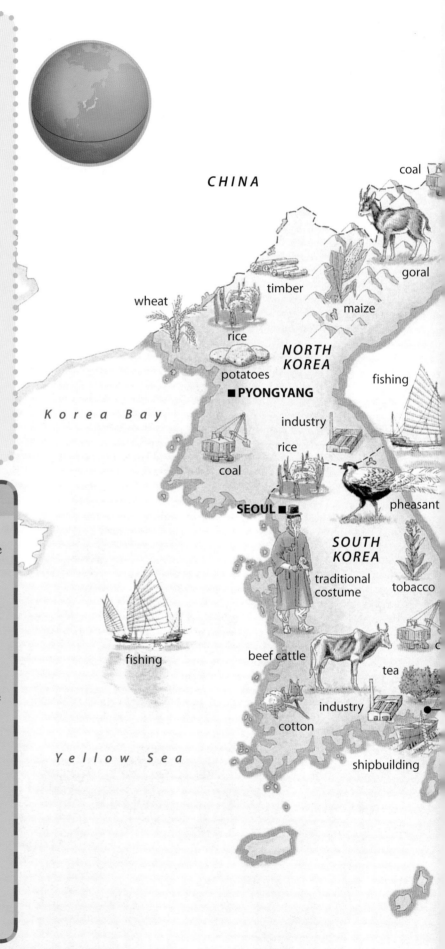

CHINA

coal

goral

timber

wheat

maize

rice

NORTH KOREA

potatoes

fishing

■ PYONGYANG

Korea Bay

industry

rice

coal

pheasant

SEOUL ■

SOUTH KOREA

traditional costume

tobacco

fishing

beef cattle

tea

industry

cotton

Yellow Sea

shipbuilding

More About...

 May 5th is Children's Day in Japan, when many families fly brightly coloured **carp streamers**. These fish-shaped wind socks are tied to bamboo poles outside homes.

 The ancient art of **sumo wrestling** is the national sport of Japan. Sumo wrestlers are very strong, and usually weigh over 150 kilograms.

 The **Ainu** were the first people to live on the islands of Japan. Today they live only on Hokkaidō island.

 The Shinkansen, or **bullet train**, is the fastest train service in Japan. With a top speed of 300 kilometres per hour, it is the world's busiest high-speed train line.

 Macaques are wild monkeys that live in Japan's snowy mountains. On very cold days, the macaques keep warm by bathing in water from hot springs.

 The famous **Torii Gate** at Miyajima rises 16 metres from the sea. It marks the entrance to a Shinto shrine.

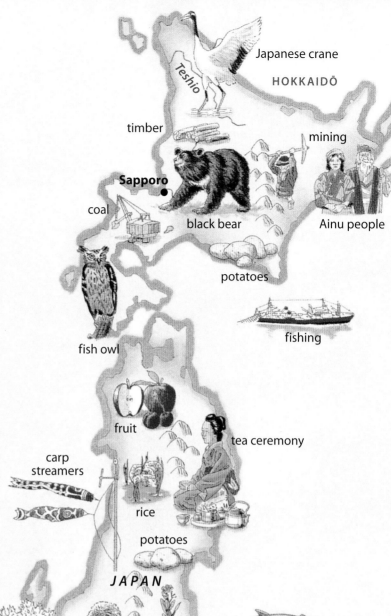

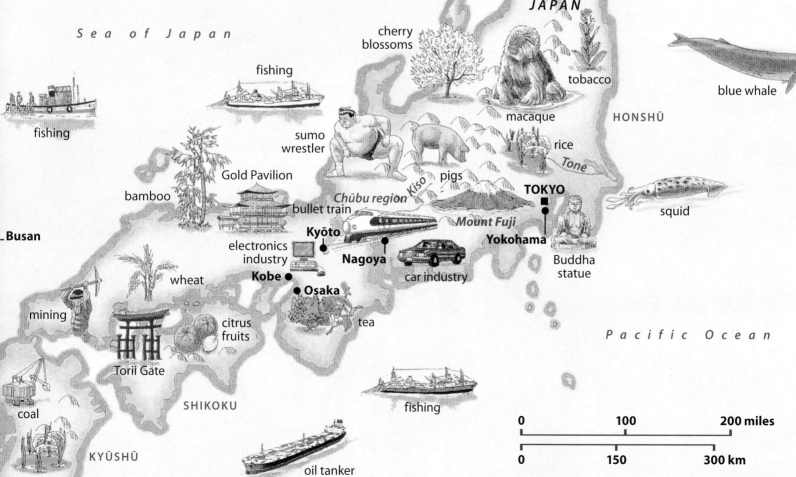

Japanese crane

HOKKAIDŌ

timber

mining

Sapporo

coal

black bear

Ainu people

potatoes

fishing

fish owl

fruit

tea ceremony

carp streamers

rice

potatoes

J A P A N

cherry blossoms

tobacco

blue whale

macaque

HONSHŪ

Sea of Japan

fishing

rice

Tone

fishing

sumo wrestler

pigs

squid

Gold Pavilion

bamboo

Chūbu region

Kiso

pigs

TOKYO

Busan

bullet train

Mount Fuji

Yokohama

electronics industry

Kyōto

Nagoya

Buddha statue

wheat

Kobe

car industry

mining

Osaka

citrus fruits

tea

Pacific Ocean

Torii Gate

coal

SHIKOKU

fishing

| 0 | 100 | 200 miles |

| 0 | 150 | 300 km |

KYŪSHŪ

rice

oil tanker

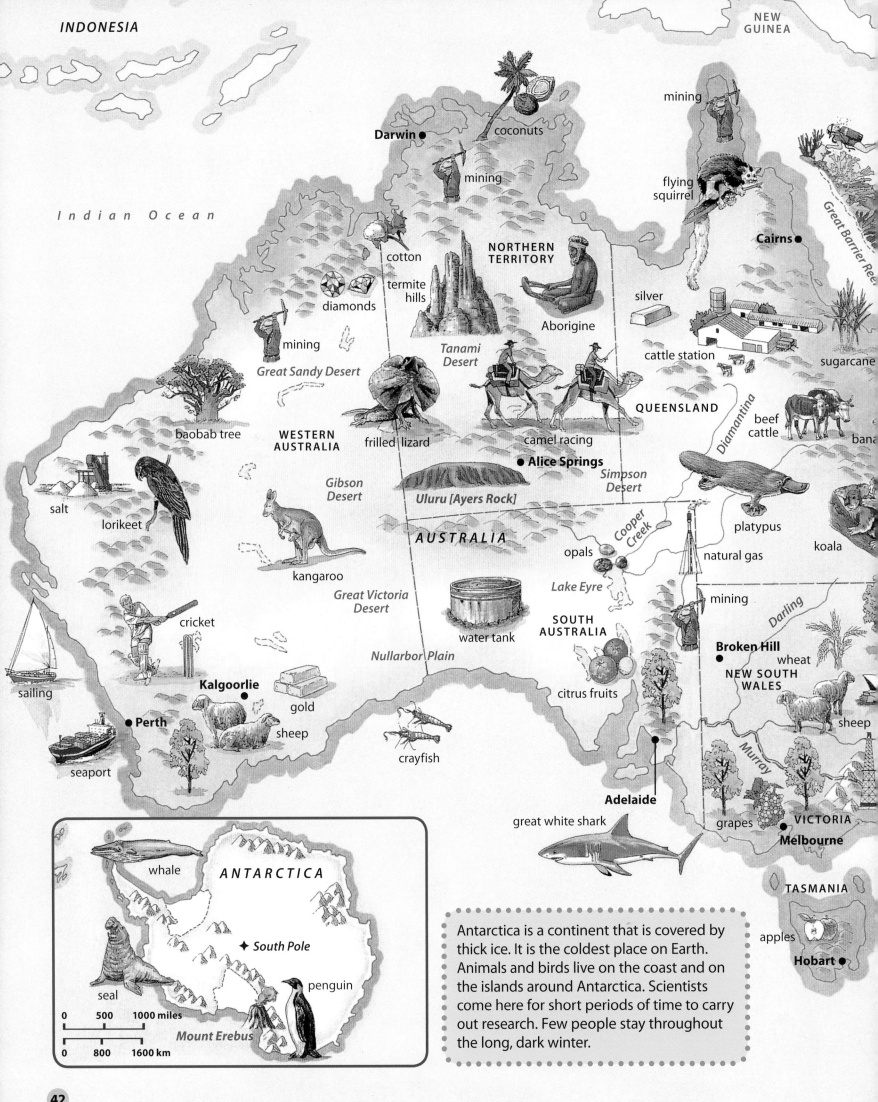

INDONESIA

NEW GUINEA

Indian Ocean

Darwin •

coconuts

mining

mining

flying squirrel

Cairns •

Great Barrier Reef

cotton

NORTHERN TERRITORY

silver

diamonds

termite hills

Aborigine

cattle station

mining

Tanami Desert

sugarcane

Great Sandy Desert

camel racing

QUEENSLAND

beef cattle

bana

baobab tree

WESTERN AUSTRALIA

frilled lizard

Alice Springs •

Diamantina

salt

Gibson Desert

Uluru [Ayers Rock]

Simpson Desert

platypus

lorikeet

opals

Cooper Creek

natural gas

koala

AUSTRALIA

kangaroo

Great Victoria Desert

Lake Eyre

cricket

water tank

SOUTH AUSTRALIA

mining

Darling

Broken Hill •

wheat

sailing

Nullarbor Plain

Kalgoorlie •

gold

citrus fruits

NEW SOUTH WALES

Perth •

sheep

sheep

seaport

crayfish

Adelaide

Murray

great white shark

grapes

VICTORIA

Melbourne •

TASMANIA

apples

Hobart •

whale

ANTARCTICA

✦ _South Pole_

seal

penguin

| 0 | 500 | 1000 miles |

| 0 | 800 | 1600 km |

Mount Erebus

Antarctica is a continent that is covered by thick ice. It is the coldest place on Earth. Animals and birds live on the coast and on the islands around Antarctica. Scientists come here for short periods of time to carry out research. Few people stay throughout the long, dark winter.

Australasia and Antarctica

Australia and New Zealand are part of the region of Australasia. Much of western Australia is hot desert and few people live there. The largest cities are along the eastern coast, where the climate is cooler. Sydney, Australia's biggest city, is home to over four million people. In the centre of Australia is the outback, a dry, hot grassland where sheep are raised. Australia is the world's principal wool producer. Farming and mining are important, too. Rich deposits of minerals, such as gold, silver, gemstones and iron are found here.

New Zealand is southeast of Australia and has a milder climate. It is divided into two main islands – North Island and South Island. Most New Zealanders live on North Island, where there are more large cities. South Island has good grazing land and dairy farming is important there.

More About...

Kangaroos belong to a group of animals called marsupials. Marsupials have pouches of skin in which their babies are carried after they are born.

Almost all the world's **opals** come from Australia, where they were first discovered in 1849. The valuable gemstones have been mined ever since.

The Maoris, descended from the first settlers in New Zealand, are known for their rich and varied culture, and particularly for fine **wood carvings**.

The **kiwi** lives in the forests of New Zealand. This odd-looking, flightness bird uses its long bill to dig for worms and grubs.

The **Great Barrier Reef** is the biggest coral reef in the world. It runs along the Queensland coast for over 2,000 kilometres. The reef is very popular with divers, but climate change and growing numbers of visitors threaten the fragile ecosystem.

Every two years the English and Australian **cricket** teams compete to win the Ashes trophy.

Did You Know?

◆ Before Europeans arrived in 1770, Australia was populated by the Aboriginal people. They had roamed the continent, hunting and gathering food, for at least 30,000 years. The land is still sacred to them. Their legend about its creation is called Dreamtime.

◆ Uluru, or Ayers Rock, rises 348 metres above the central Australian desert. To the Aboriginal people, this vast red rock is a sacred place. At the rock's base are caves, which have paintings on the walls.

◆ The Maori name for New Zealand is Aotearoa, which means 'land of the long white cloud'.

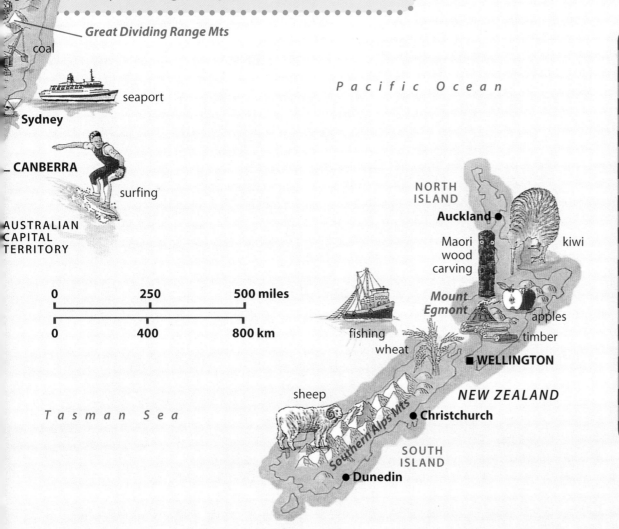

bacco

Brisbane

grapes

Great Dividing Range Mts

coal

Pacific Ocean

seaport

Sydney

surfing

CANBERRA

AUSTRALIAN
CAPITAL
TERRITORY

0	250	500 miles
0	400	800 km

NORTH
ISLAND

Auckland ●

Maori
wood
carving

kiwi

*Mount
Egmont*

apples

fishing

timber

wheat

■ **WELLINGTON**

sheep

Southern Alps Mts

● **Christchurch**

NEW ZEALAND

Tasman Sea

SOUTH
ISLAND

● **Dunedin**

Glossary

canal
A man-made waterway constructed for the transport of goods by water or for travel.

canyon
A large valley with steep sides, cut into the earth over many hundreds of years by flowing water, such as a river.

capital
The city where a country's government is located.

civilization
A society (group of people) that has developed to a high level of organisation and culture.

climate
The type of weather that is usual in a particular place.

continent
A very large area of land, usually made up of many countries. The Earth has seven continents.

crop
Plants that are grown specially for sale or use, such as for food or making material for clothes. Grains, cotton, vegetables and fruit are crops.

desert
A place where little rain falls. Deserts can be hot or cold. Few plants can grow in deserts.

dialect
The way that people speak in a particular area that is different or unique.

economy
The buying, selling and production of goods and services.

famine
A severe shortage of food in a particular place. A famine might be a result of bad weather or war.

gorge
A valley with steep sides, cut into the earth by flowing water, such as a river. A canyon is a large gorge.

industry
The making and selling of goods, such as clothes, cars or toys.

inhabitant
A person who lives in a particular place, such as a city or region.

kilometre
A measurement of distance that is 1,000 metres long. A kilometre is the same as 0.6 miles.

metre
A measurement of distance or height. A metre is 100 centimetres long. A doorway is usually about 2 metres tall.

mile
A measurement of distance. A mile is the same as 1.6 kilometres.

natural resource
A naturally occurring source of goods that can be used or sold, such as timber, water or coal.

plain
A large, flat area of land covered with grass with few trees.

plantation
A large farm where crops are grown.

population
All the people who live in a specific place, such as a town, region or country.

rainforest
A dense tropical forest where it rains heavily throughout the year.

refugee
Someone who has had to leave the place where they live in order to find food or safety.

region
A large area of land. A region might have particular features, such as mountains or forests.

religion
A set of beliefs about how the universe was made and how people should behave.

republic
A country that is not ruled by a king or queen. A republic is usually ruled by a president.

savanna
A large, flat area of land covered in coarse grass.

spice
A dried part of a plant that is used in cooking to give food a particular taste or smell. Pepper, cinnamon, paprika and nutmeg are spices.

subtropical
Regions that are located next to the tropics are called subtropical.

sultan
The ruler of an Islamic (Muslim) country.

swamp
A low area of wetland that is usually covered by water.

temple
A special building where people go to worship.

terrain
An area of land, often with specific features, such as rocky or flat ground.

tomb
A room or chamber in which a dead person's body is buried.

tropics
The hot regions found either side of the equator, called the Tropic of Cancer (to the north) and the Tropic of Capricorn (to the south). Somewhere in, or something from, the tropics can be described as **tropical**.

valley
Low-lying land between mountains or hills. A valley will often have a river or stream running through it.

volcano
A mountain or hill, usually topped by a crater, through which hot molten rock (lava) is pushed up from under the surface of the earth.

Map Index

 Kyrgyzstan

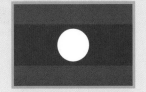 Laos

 Latvia

 Lebanon

 Lesotho

 Liberia

 Malawi

 Malaysia

 Mali

 Malta

 Mauritania

 Mauritius

 Mozambique

 Myanmar / Burma

 Namibia

 Nepal

 Netherlands

 New Zealand

 Pakistan

 Panama

 Papua New Guinea

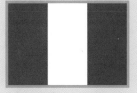 Paraguay

 Peru

 Philippines

 Russia

 Rwanda

 Saint Kitts and Nevis

 Saint Lucia

Saint Vincent and the Grenadines

San Marino

 Slovakia

 Slovenia

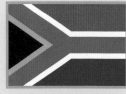 Somalia

 South Africa

 South Korea

South Sudan

 Switzerland

 Syria

 Tajikistan

 Tanzania

 Thailand

 Togo

 United Arab Emirates

 United Kingdom

 United States of America

 Uruguay

 Uzbekistan

 Vatican City